Building Healthy Organizations

Building Healthy Organizations

Transforming organizations through values based leadership

The BHO Group

Foreword by Dr. Carson Pue, Arrow Leadership

Published by The BHO Group at Computronix

Suite 200, 10216-124 Street, Edmonton, Alberta, Canada T5N 4A3

Readers should be aware that Internet Web sites offered as citations and/or sources for further information may have changed or disappeared between the time this was written and when it is read.

Order this book online at www.trafford.com
or email orders@trafford.com

Most Trafford titles are also available at major online book retailers.

Printed in Victoria, BC, Canada.

ISBN: 978-1-4269-2282-4 (sc)
ISBN: 978-1-4269-2293-0 (hc)

Library of Congress Control Number: 2009912307

Our mission is to effi ciently provide the world's fi nest, most comprehensive book publishing service, enabling every author to experience success. To fi nd out how to publish your book, your way, and have it available worldwide, visit us online at www.traff ord.com

Trafford rev. 11/13/09

 www.trafford.com

North America & International
toll-free: 1 888 232 4444 (USA & Canada)
phone: 250 383 6864 ♦ fax: 812 355 4082

"It's impossible to overstate the importance of building a healthy organization. From the boardroom to the work station, it's as fundamental as oxygen is to our existence. I'm jazzed about *Building Healthy Organizations* because its combination of captivating real-life stories and practical application steps make the book both readable and actionable. The Five V.A.L.U.E. System will guide leaders in their decision making, which will in turn yield significantly in the health of their organizations."

Jim Brown
Bestselling author of *The Imperfect Board Member*

"On a personal level, this book has restored my commitment as CEO to build a strong, healthy, and well balanced leadership team that actively shares, communicates, and demonstrates the organization's cultural and operational vision to all staff."

Lynn Groves Hautmann
President/CEO - Chrysalis

"In the business world where marketing, manufacturing, and intellectual property are so important and so pursued, it is refreshing to read a book that says we are worth more than what we are saying, doing, and knowing; our true importance is our being. Whether we are employees of a company, part of the management team, or visionary leaders, this book will help build a healthy organization… and that is good for business."

Paul Richardson
President -CBMC

"It has been a pleasure working with the BHO Group. They understand what it takes to get employees engaged in a team. Today's employee needs more than a paycheck to get connected and BHO helps employers figure out how to effectively engage employees."

Peter Lacey
President & CEO - Cervus LP

Contents

Foreword

Dr. Carson Pue, Arrow Leadership

Behind every healthy organization is a healthy leader.

—Dr. John McAuley, Arrow Leadership

If you can't lead yourself, you can't lead a team.

If you can't lead a team, you can't lead an organization.

Leading a group of leaders in the competitive high-tech sector can be like trying to herd cats. Since Herman Leusink had succeeded in pulling this off, I wanted to meet the man.

When I did, I knew I was in the presence of a leader of great competence and character. He also had an obvious calling, and that was to build a business that was healthy—a place where people mattered.

Over the years, I have read several volumes on the subject of organization development. It is interesting to note the authors are seldom the people actually charged with doing it. Often the writers are consultants or academics. *Building Healthy Organizations* is grounded in the fact that its authors are actually doing it. I have been to their offices and know the principal leaders there. Every word found within this book is accurate—and the wisdom shared here works.

Leaders need all the help they can get to lead teams and organizations. This book's plain, sensible approach is simple without being simplistic. It is lucid and clear, with the crispness of the winter Alberta air, where its thoughts and ideas were germinated. If you are a leader concerned about building your organization or business into a healthier environment, this is a very useful volume. My dream is that businesses and organizations will "get it" and intentionally work towards making our places of work healthy in every respect. Who wouldn't want to work at a place like that?

Dr. Carson Pue
President/CEO Arrow Leadership
Author of Best Selling book "Mentoring Leaders"

Preface

Building Healthy Organizations is the result of thirty years of treating people with respect, trust, and a serving attitude at a successful North American high-tech company called Computronix, which has offices in Edmonton, Alberta, and Denver, Colorado. In 1979, President and CEO Herman Leusink was tired of working for organizations that treated people more like "human doings" than like "human beings." He believed that if he treated people with value and respect, they would be more likely to contribute meaningfully to the company than if he treated them as part of the machinery.

Thirty years of experience has proved his philosophy. A healthy environment produces growth in people and profits, engagement in staff and clients, and an opportunity for owners to develop a legacy that outlives their tenure. Computronix has an annual turnover rate of around 5 percent, and absenteeism is less than 50 percent of industry norms. That would be an enviable record in most businesses but it's an almost-impossible dream in the world of technology and computer systems. Internally, staff report high satisfaction levels, a large percentage of new staff are referred by present employees, a significant part of the staff has been with Computronix for more than a decade. During hard times, when product research costs were especially high, staff believed in the vision and gave up paychecks or held them for later. Staff share with each other when needs arise, contributing to help offset unexpected personal costs when one of them hits a tough spot in life.

Many staff bring parents and friends through the office for a tour to meet their colleagues and see where they work. Photographs of employees and their families hang along the halls of the offices. It's more than team building and nice people—it's a system *relentlessly held as core to the Computronix competitive position*. The company is passionate about "building healthy people."

Over the years, Herman has mentored and trained many leaders and supervisors in the art of treating people well, both inside Computronix and in other organizations he's been involved with. His experience led him to ask: Is there a recipe for achieving what many observers referred to as a leading-edge healthy organization? Is there architecture to his approach? Can other organizations benefit from it?

In 2005, after much internal research and study, we made a breakthrough discovery as the correlation between values, principles, and practices became apparent as a key ingredient in Herman's approach. A core set of values acting in the tension of paradox jumped off the pages of our research. There in front of us was a moving engine working in harmony that provided the power to drive a healthy organization. The cylinders were the values applied to all staff decisions, budget investments, and staff and policy development. The paradox living above each value were like valves opening and closing, allowing a complex mixture of ideas and decisions to travel through the engine, producing a powerful torque that for thirty years has delivered on workplace health. Although Herman had intuitively discovered what worked, he had not yet described it. The work began to blueprint the engine and all its moving parts.

With the clarity achieved by developing the blueprint and the belief that it should be shared with others to power them forward to their own vision of a healthy organization, the Building Healthy Organizations (BHO) Group at Computronix was born. The principles and values that drove Computronix (what we've since come to call the BHO DNA) began to be taught in other organizations, with similar impact and success.

We were nervous as we left the safety of our own organization. Our engine had never been tested on the open road. What's happened since 2005 has been astounding. In place after place, with person after person, we began to see the lights come on for many leaders and staff. Presidents, CEOs, VPs, and other leaders recognized the truths of the values, principles, and practices. Class surveys collected by a leading college gave us courage through comments like, "This is the best material I've seen in ten years!" and, "Why didn't I learn these concepts twenty years ago?" and, "When can you come and share this with our organization?"

The blueprint represents a whole new approach to driving people practices forward. This isn't just HR, leadership, or culture. This is a framework for building structures to promote best-in-class organizations. This is an engagement framework that honors people and balances their needs with the practical needs of a business. Our clients validate the framework with story after story from their own journeys, confirming the importance of each of the values that drive organizational health. In classes and leadership retreats, people not only "get it," but also can internalize the framework quickly to develop more health in their own organizations. More than the message, it's also been the mental exercise and increased self-awareness our clients enjoy as they wrestle with the paradoxes contained in each value system. Common sense shows up, and clarity for resolving age old staff issues is achieved.

Leadership teams openly joke with one another as they discover the biases the Workplace Relationship Indicator (WRI) tool highlights as it clarifies the paradoxes that exist with each value system. Leaders realize that they can profile and balance their own values. We hear it over and over, "I see why my thinking leads to some of the issues on my team. Finally, I have a diagnostic tool that highlights the real problem."

By 2008, we felt that it was time to write a book to detail the framework and ideas so it could be shared on a much broader scale. The book you now hold in your hands is a description of the values and principles that we've learned. We trust that it will help you to bring the principles of healthy organization into your company, department, and team, as well as into your own life.

Acknowledgments

The "we" in this book is the BHO Group, a team of consultants that have formed around the vision of transplanting the BHO DNA from Computronix to other companies that want to treat people well. Broadly, "we" refers to every consultant, trainer, and co-worker at Computronix who has had a hand in creating, defining, and sharing this framework solution with other organizations. Specifically, "we" is Stephen Brown, Ron den Otter, David Neumann, and John Wiseman, the team who wrote *Building Healthy Organizations*.

We would specifically like to thank the leadership teams at Cervus LP, Cormode and Dickson, and Chrysalis for their many insights and contributions to the work. In each organization, we have been impressed with the commitment to treat staff with a balanced perspective, and their belief in our work has made it possible for this book to be written.

The Operations Management Team at Computronix has been highly supportive of the project. Their belief in what we were doing allowed us to build the BHO Group, and they've been absolutely committed to getting the message into print.

Finally, the book is a tribute to Herman Leusink's input into our lives, and the lives of so many others. We are deeply grateful for the growth that he has inspired in us, and we hope that reading *Building Healthy Organizations* will help you to experience some of that same inspiration.

Introduction

In the fall of 2005, Warren Shepell, an international human resource services provider and research organization, said unhealthy job environments are a leading cause of psychological withdrawal, poor effort, lateness, absence, and staff turnover. They published research that showed that the effect on profitability can easily be between 15 percent and 20 percent of pretax profit. In effect, healthy organizations have the opportunity to dramatically increase their bottom line by focusing on the factors that affect organizational health.[1]

There is a large body of research showing that subjective workplace factors have twice the impact of the objective factors on workplace health. That means that pay, benefits, and working conditions are only half as important for job satisfaction as the softer aspects of culture and relationships with co-workers and managers.

Your organization competes with others for top-notch employees as much as it does for market share and customer dollars. Once you recruit and engage those top-notch employees, you have to maintain your investment in them or risk losing them to a competitor when they become disillusioned or otherwise dissatisfied with the work environment. The cost of replacing employees can easily be double their annual wage once recruiting, training, and engagement costs are counted.

When you ask employees what leaders do to lose their trust, you get some interesting answers. The category that gets the highest response is frustration with leaders who say one thing and do another. Following that are the leaders who put their own interests ahead of the interests of the team or the organization. Third place goes to the leaders who withhold information from their staff or teams to maintain a certain degree of control. It's rare to find someone who can't relate to one of these categories—almost everyone has worked for a boss who fits one of those descriptions. While there are people who are dissatisfied with their jobs because they feel they aren't paid enough or the benefits plan is too stingy, it's rare for people to cite those more tangible things as the reason they're looking for a new employer.

When you ask employees who love their jobs just what it is that makes them feel so positive, the answers don't usually have anything to do with wages or benefits either. Trust is at the top of most people's lists; they feel they can trust their managers and supervisors, all the way up the chain to the owners or executives. Feeling valued or listened to is high on the list as well. Satisfied staff feel that when they have something to say, there's someone who's willing to listen and put some value on what they contribute. They feel they have input into decisions that are likely to affect them.

> *The dream is to have an environment that's so healthy and attractive that people will do almost anything to get hired by your organization.*

Obviously, understanding how to create an environment of trust and respect, where people feel that they are welcome and valuable members of the team, is important. Failing to do so is not only expensive, but also makes it impossible to continue doing business over time. The dream is to have an environment that's so healthy and attractive that people will do almost anything to get hired by your organization and maintain that same high level of commitment and engagement as they work with you and for you for decades. The dream turns to a nightmare when you have to compete with someone who has better people than you do, especially if you're investing the training dollars to get those people up to speed, and your competitor is happily hiring them when they get tired of your workplace environment.

How does an organization deal with the subjective or "soft" side of its culture and its work environment? Can organizations find ways to quantify, measure, and manage those things? Can they find ways to help employees deal with increasing stress and pressure in ways that *increase* organizational health instead of *diminishing* it?

When people and organizations react to stress and pressure, they do so based on an underlying set of values rather than on the discipline of following prescribed policy and procedure. This means organizations face something of a dilemma: they are confronted with the reality that developing commonly held values and employee character are critical to their ability to sustain a healthy culture and thus a healthy competitive position. At the same time, they have little in the way of tools or methods to help them facilitate that values & character development.

To date, we've found that the tools and methods that do exist are woefully inadequate. Almost by definition, character qualities are defined by their failure point, not by their strength. There has to be a better way. We need a way to understand how to measure the underlying variables that create a healthy organization. We need to be able to identify the fundamental building blocks of an organization's culture and work environment and find ways to measure those things. Most important, we need to find ways to manage those things in a way that helps us *proactively* define and develop a healthy organization; build a healthy workplace on purpose—by design.

We believe we've found such a tool—a set of objective measurements that helps define organizational health. We know that it works, because we're using it successfully in a number of different environments and with a wide variety of people. As you read through this book and begin to apply the values and tools that we have discovered, we trust that your organization will experience the same success that Computronix has enjoyed over the last 30 years.

How This Book Is Organized

This book is organized into three sections that deal with the five BHO V.A.L.U.E.'s at three different levels. The first section, Defining Organizational Health, presents a high-level, conceptual overview of the five values. The second section, Building Healthy Organizations, makes the value systems practical and discusses the way that the values impact workplace health. The third section, Maintaining Organizational Health, presents tools and best practices for building health into your own workplace.

**Defining Organizational Disease -
High level concepts**

• What is health?
• What are the 5 value systems?

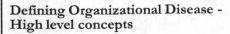

**Building Healthy Organizations -
Practical help**

• Finding the balance that works
• Organizational checkup - Employee
  surveys, Self Awareness
• Value system alignment - Leaders,
  Culture, Staff

**Maintaining Organizational Health -
Tools and best practices**

• Promoting the values
• Building a healthy culture
• Define the principles before the policies

If *Building Healthy Organizations* helps you with tools and systems for measuring and managing health in your organization or with the teams that you lead, then we've accomplished at least part of our purpose in writing the book. If you're inspired to think more deeply about the value systems that shape your worldview and your leadership style and how that affects the people around you, then we will feel as though our effort has been well worth it.

Section 1
Defining Organizational Health

Understanding an Organization's Pain Points

"Organizational pain" is an interesting metaphor. But what is it, exactly? How do we define it and measure it? We've all experienced it. Dysfunction and discomfort at work that expresses itself in terms of low commitment, lack of trust, disrespect, confusion about responsibilities and expectations, low productivity—the list goes on and on. Staff members in those organizations don't stick around long—almost any excuse will do to stay away from work—and they definitely don't recommend the company to their friends!

But the concept leaves many questions unanswered. If unhealthy organizations experience pain, can it be treated? Is the treatment effective? Does the patient recover? Or is it more like minimizing discomfort? Can the pain be prevented in the first place? Is there some sort of process that an organization can follow to monitor its health—like an annual checkup—and then take steps to treat dysfunction before it becomes a problem? How effective is the treatment? Does it take hold immediately, or is it a long, unpleasant process? Is the treatment worse than the problem, or does it provide relief quickly?

Like pain in our bodies, there can be different causes for pain in unhealthy organizations. When we experience pain in our bodies, we don't need a doctor to tell us that something is wrong. A doctor should be able to tell us exactly *what* is wrong, and how to treat it effectively, but the pain itself tells us that something is not working as it should. Machines don't feel pain like people do, but the concept still holds— excess wear and breakdown are signs that something in the design is not quite right. An engineer should be able to tell us exactly what is causing the problem and how it can be fixed, but the fact that wear or breakdown *exists* tells us that something is amiss.

Organizations share that characteristic. When things aren't working right, when there's a problem with how they're designed and how the parts are interacting with each other, they experience pain, excess wear, and breakdown. We might not be able to pinpoint the specifics with accuracy, but we know by feel that something isn't right. And like the doctor and the engineer, when we have the right diagnostic tools and knowledge, we should be able to identify *what* isn't working and *why*.

If there are unhealthy organizations, then surely there are healthy ones too. Places where people respect and trust one another, where they are committed to each other and to the company, where there's good balance between work and other needs, and where they're so excited about working together that they virtually drag their friends and relatives into the boss' office, hoping that there will be a job for them too. A dream? Maybe. More like a vision, perhaps.

The National Institute for Occupational Safety & Health (NIOSH) in the United States defines a healthy organization as one whose culture, climate, and practices create an environment that promotes employee health and safety as well as organizational effectiveness.[2]

The World Health Organization (WHO) said in their 1999 guideline for developing healthy workplaces:

> A healthy workplace is a place where everyone works together to achieve an agreed vision for the health and well-being of workers and the surrounding community. It provides all members of the workforce with physical, psychological, social, and organizational conditions that protect and promote health and safety. It enables managers and workers to increase control over their own

2

health and to improve it, and to become more energetic, positive, and contented. In return, the workforce is more stable, committed, and productive.[3]

Here's our definition, and it's the one that we'll use throughout the rest of this book:

A healthy organization is a productive organization where respect, trust, and service flourish.

The next chapters delve into the values that define a healthy organization.

Chapter 1: What are Values?

Every one of us has a value system that shapes who we are. The decisions we make every day are guided by our values. Some of those decisions are deliberate and easy to explain. Some are difficult to articulate, because they're related to intuitive, gut-feel reactions. Companies have value systems that shape how they do business and treat their customers and employees. Communities have value systems that establish what's accepted as "normal" and dictate how people are expected to behave around one another.

Building Healthy Organizations is about discovering the value systems that shape the interactions between the people who make up an organization. Initially, we wondered if this should be a book about *individual* value systems or about *corporate* value systems. It seemed like it was an important question, but in the end, we're not sure that it makes a difference. Why? Watch a leadership change take place in a company. Notice that it doesn't take long before the company seems to pick up the personality of the new leader; a strong leader's personal values are quickly adopted by the organization. When there's a clash between the new leader's values and the values already entrenched in the organization, there are big changes coming! People who can't embrace the new values become more and more uncomfortable, their stress levels go up, and they become unhappy. They might become so unhappy that they leave or so irritating that they're dismissed, or they might just sit there like a festering sore that needs attention. When new leaders aren't strong enough to survive the transition period and instill their values into the organization, they will be the ones who experience increasing stress and either leave or fester.

Where value systems match, people will find that they fit. The less their value systems match, the more discomfort they experience. When there's little in common, there's little to provide a bond. People who don't share the same values misunderstand each other's actions and often end up in conflict.

Understanding Values

Individually, people express their value systems in a different way than organizations do. Our personal values are a collection of preferences, beliefs, and boundaries that shape our decision making and help define our responses to pressure or stress. An organization's values are expressed in the policies, principles, and expectations that direct the behavior of its employees.

Preferences

Preferences are things that are pretty much negotiable. All of us have ways that we'd like things to be done and ways that we'd like people to relate to us. For the most part, we're pretty flexible about these things. Preferences can change over time with the slightest motivation. One day, we discover a different soft drink in the machine down the hall, and we have a new favorite! Sometimes we change our preferences on purpose—if we discover that we need to adjust our preferences to suit someone else's style, we can make that sacrifice with a little effort. That's not to say that preferences aren't important—they are. They tell us quite a bit about ourselves, but they're not very deeply rooted. More important, they are rarely the underlying cause of conflict nor are they the glue that bonds us to others.

> *Organizations express their preferences by writing policies.*

Organizations have preferences that are described by their *policies*. Policies, in effect, spell out how the organization wants its staff to act in a given situation. Like a person's preferences, an organization's policies are important, but they do change over time. A new situation comes up, and a revision to the policy comes out to address it.

Beliefs

Our personal beliefs go much deeper than our preferences. *Beliefs* are some of the building blocks that define who we are and why we do what we do. Beliefs have a profound impact on our character, outlook on life, and reactions to life's bumps and surprises. Consider how our beliefs define our answers to life's difficult questions: Where do we come from? Why are we here? What happens to us when we die? Why do things happen the way they do?

Beliefs aren't necessarily based on facts. Sometimes they have more to do with perception than reality. For example, a person might be perfectly capable of doing something. They have the aptitude, skill, and strength to do it. But, *if they believe that they can't do it*, then, *for them*, that belief becomes reality: they can't do it. Belief becomes a limiting factor. It works the other way too. People do amazing things just because they believe they can, without any experience, training, or apparent qualification, because "I just knew I could!"

While beliefs are close to values, they're still not the foundational building blocks of our character. Beliefs change over time. We grow, experience, and try things. Repeated failure has a way of making us believe that what we'd hoped to do is impossible. On the other hand, success has a way of expanding our horizons and making us believe that a whole new arena of possibility exists where we'd previously seen limitations. Beliefs shape our faith, self-image, and ability to trust and love. What we believe can either empower us or hold us back.

Principles define what an organization believes.

Organizations have beliefs too, but they're expressed by the *principles* that guide decision-makers. Often those principles, like a person's beliefs, aren't written down anywhere—they're a commonly held ideology that shapes the way the organization writes its policies and expresses its goals, but they're difficult to articulate or describe. Leaders in an organization are referring to principles when they talk about the way the organization likes to do things or when they make choices about what they will and won't embrace as goals.

Values

Most of us have a lot of preferences. We also have a lot of beliefs. But, we have surprisingly few values. And it's rare to be able to articulate our values without first having discovered them in the crucible of life—in those times where we're forced by life's circumstance to get down to the bare essentials. Those are the times where we discover the things that we absolutely will not change.

Values are the fundamental building blocks of character that outline who we really are inside—what makes us unique. For the most part, values involve our interaction with people. They're the internal rules that tell us how to treat ourselves and others. The physical world around us never gets in the way like people do—we can drill holes through mountains, find ways to adapt to extremes of climate or geography, and even escape gravity and leave the earth itself. Those aren't the main things that prevent us from reaching our goals—often, it's a clash with people in our lives. We've all experienced the challenge of a difficult relationship. Sometimes, it doesn't even have to be an intimate or long-lasting relationship that challenges us. Even shallow or casual relationships get in our way sometimes; people we don't have to interact with very often can affect us significantly.

> *If values are out of sync with priorities, actions will fall short of intentions.*

Understanding values is very practical. Setting personal priorities, and having the discipline to stick with them, can't be done successfully until we know something about our values. If our values are out of sync with our priorities, our actions will continually fall short of our intentions. Our consciences will bother us incessantly if our jobs or positions require us to contradict a value—people can become depressed, angry, or cynical trying to handle the conflict.

Our values rarely change. When they do, it's usually out of some very difficult experience—the kind of experience that leaves us questioning our purpose in life or that leaves us searching for ways to ensure that we learn the lesson and never have to repeat the exercise that brought us to that point again. Because they're at the root of the way that we think, changing our values often shifts the entire structure of our lives. When values change, people who know us say things like, "What happened to you? You've changed!" Their tone of voice can be positive or negative—we can change for the better or for the worse.

Think for a minute about water building up in the reservoir behind a dam. Slowly, the buildup of water puts more and more pressure on the dam, until one of two things happens. Either the dam holds, the reservoir is full, and everything works as designed, or the dam gives way and the reservoir gushes through the break, wreaking havoc on everything in its way. Our values are like that dam—they form immovable boundaries in our lives. Slowly the pressures of life build up behind them, and either they prove to be strong enough to hold, or they give way dramatically, allowing the pressure behind them to come crashing through the foundations of our lives, tearing at our very souls. When things settle down, we make one of two decisions after we evaluate the results: either we rebuild the dam, strengthening a value so that it will hold more securely next time, or we change, deciding that the principles by which we live our lives need to be adjusted. In the real world, we can all relate to what those decisions sound like. When we decide to rebuild and entrench a value even more deeply, our thoughts run along the lines of, "I will never let anyone do that to me again," or "I will never let myself get put into that position again." When we decide that the value isn't a hill that's worth dying on, we sigh and think "I guess that just doesn't really matter to me after all."

Organizations have values too—systems of thinking that lie at their core. Those values define the principles that guide the way they operate and the policies by which they manage the actions and decisions of their staff. When the values in an organization are built on poor foundations, there can be enormous repercussions. How many of the ethical and financial disasters of the last twenty years were a result of corrupt value systems? How much damage was caused by the collapse of the organization when the values that should have held everything in check gave way and released a torrent of destruction into the society that should have been the beneficiary of their efforts?

The values of an organization are set by the people who give it leadership and direction. As leaders, our values shape the culture and environment that forms around us.

Discovering V.A.L.U.E.

What we need is a way to objectively identify a person's or an organization's values, and be able to predict where the conflicts between them will be. If we could point to a value that an organization (or its leaders) hold and identify employees who either share or don't share that same value, we could predict which employees are likely to get into conflict with the organization as well as what that conflict will be about. We could work that understanding into hiring practices so we focus on recruiting people who are likely to fit well. We could use that knowledge to point out the inconsistencies between our vision statements and how we *really* act—the inconsistencies that create discontent and cynicism among the staff within an organization. On a personal level, we could discover the values in our own lives, find ways to assess their merit, strengthen those we feel are good, and make significant changes where we see a need for growth.

How many different areas are there where we can form values? Dozens? Hundreds? Take a look through most of the helpful books on leadership and management. Most of them focus on three or four specific concepts or activities—sometimes five or six but rarely more. As much as we like to think we're infinitely complex as human beings, the reality is that we really can't do a good job of focusing on more than a few things at once. We think that same logic applies to understanding values. Because values shape how we live at such a foundational level, it's likely that there aren't more than a handful that we really have to think about.

We believe there are five areas where we form values that affect the health of our workplace relationships. Each of these values relates to how we interact with people. The five values form the acrostic V.A.L.U.E. While they are discussed further in the following chapters, asking these questions can help you begin to define each one.

1) **Value:** Is a person's value largely based on what they can do for us or help us do? Or, do we have a way of understanding their value, independent of what they do to benefit us?

2) **Aptitude:** Is it our primary responsibility to assign tasks and "get the job done?" Or, do we have a responsibility for recognizing, cultivating, and developing people's gifts and abilities?

3) **Learning:** How do we perceive the mentoring or coaching part of our role? Are we primarily focused on honing job skills, or are we responsible to press people to grow?

4) **Unity:** In a conflict of priorities, do we sacrifice our own needs to meet the expectations of others? Do we tend to prioritize our own agenda, expecting others to live by our rules? Can people live as healthy members of a community while continuing to meet legitimate personal needs?

5) **Empathy:** How do we respond to people who need help? Do we feel that people should be held accountable for the way they use the gifts we give, or do we trust that people who are "victims of circumstance" will make responsible choices with those gifts?

In looking at these questions, we need to understand the idea of paradox. By definition, a paradox exists when two mutually exclusive things or ideas must coexist. In theory, the two things simply can't exist at the same time—in reality, they do. Our sense of justice, perspective of others, cultural baseline in terms of faith or religion, socioeconomic status, and lots of other factors will affect how we see the choices at each end of the spectrum painted by the question. But, we need to resist the urge to presume that these questions have a "right or wrong" or a "good and evil" context. For the most part, they don't. There is some context in which an extreme position on any one of the questions might be wrong, but remember that the questions are intended to describe a paradox, not to give an either-or choice. In fact, the only way to balance the paradox is to find a place where we can reasonably embrace a fairly wide set of choices.

The Road Ahead

The next few chapters will put each of these values on a continuum—a range of choices that stretch from one extreme to the other. Each scale represents a paradox: the extremes are mutually exclusive because we can't have them both. People who hold to an extreme in their personal point of view often call those who hold to the other extreme "wrong" or "stupid." An extreme doesn't usually make for a comfortable place to live. Finding a comfortable place on the continuum is done by striking a balance between the two ends—a balance that must fit our personal value systems.

There's no magic formula that tells us exactly how to find that balance; there's no "right" way or "wrong" way. But there is a methodology to it. Instead of trying to find the specific point at which we think the system will balance, like the center point of a teeter-totter, we've got to take a broader perspective. There's a zone between the two extremes where we can find a workable solution that may not be entirely perfect but where we can live with the trade-offs, a place where we do our best to understand the perspective of those who see the world differently than we do.

In fact, if we choose to include an extreme in our embrace, we find that the center we were hoping to include is beyond our grasp. If we position ourselves near the center and reach as far left and as far right as we can, we discover that we can include a fairly diverse set of opinions and expectations and develop the widest possible basis for consensus.

The analogy we use to describe paradox is that of a country road with a ditch running along both sides. For every mile of balanced perspective, there are two miles of unbalanced, unhealthy points of view that run right along each side. These represent the extremes of the choices on the value system. What we want to do is avoid driving in the ditch—it's better to stay on the road. Whether we prefer to be on the left, right, or middle of the road is up to us. The important thing is that we keep out of the ditch!

One last thought before we get to the details. It's important to understand that we have an amazing capacity to deceive ourselves in terms of self-assessment. There's an old proverb that says in effect, "Honest self-assessment is impossible when your priority is self-preservation." We can decide what we think our values ought to be by engaging in an academic exercise or by clinging to a particular philo-sophical position. But, if we want to know what's *really* at our core, then instead of thinking about our *intentions*, we have to look critically at our actions. We must look at what we *do* and not at what we should have done or wish we had done.

Chapter 2:   Value

Understanding What People Are Worth

We are here for something new—it's not happened much in the history of the world. We are an army out to set other men free. America should be free ground, all of it, not a line divided by slave state and free—all the way from here to the Pacific Ocean. No man has to bow, no man born to royalty. Here we judge you by what you do, not by who your father was. Here you can be something; here is a place to build a home. But it's not the land—there is always more land—it's the idea that we all have value, you and me. What we are fighting for in the end is each other.

—Col. Joshua Chamberlain, 20th Maine Regiment

What are people worth—how do you assess their value? When people lack motivation, do you help them find the things that stir their passion, or do you encourage them to buy in to your passions and dreams?

For this value, the ditch on the left side of the road is called Slave Driver. It's an extreme, task-oriented, utilitarian orientation. Employers are focused purely on hitting goals and targets, even at the expense of people and relationships. Policy and procedure are primarily developed to prevent employees from taking advantage of the organization. Everything is reduced to a set of clear-cut instructions, without regard for people's feelings,

People have inherent value beyond their ability to produce or please.

15

wants, likes, and dislikes. Many toxic organizations live in this ditch.

To live in the ditch on the right side of the road is to be a People-Pleaser. It's an over-sensitive, exaggerated attempt to cater to the preferences of others. Employers become crippled by a need to please everyone. Priorities are almost impossible to establish, because everything has to go through such a long consensus-building process. This is the ditch that social services or nonprofit organizations might fall into. In their attempt to treat everyone equally, they may find themselves spread so thinly that they're unable to reach their goals.

Slave Driver (Utilitarian)	Balanced	People-Pleaser (Overly-Sensitive)
• Disloyal to people in favor of completing a task or hitting a goal. • Feeling and relationship issues poorly managed. • Evaluations focus exclusively on tasks and outcomes.	• Show appreciation for others by listening to them, and providing helpful feedback. • Relationship issues balanced with the need to reach goals. • No prejudice in dealing with mistakes—we assume people intend to do the right thing.	• Overly concerned with pleasing others. • Indecisive; change is very slow. • Difficult to establish priorities.

We've all seen companies that have them, that plaque on the reception wall that says something like, "Our greatest asset is our people." Maybe the organization you work for now has one. But what does that mean? How are people an asset? Unfortunately, most of the time the people the plaque refer to feel like that statement refers to their economic value, the utilitarian value that they bring to the economy or to the workplace. Does that plaque say that it's the people themselves who are valuable? Or that the real asset is the money people earn, the products they build, or the sales they make? We like to ask the question this way: Are people *human beings*, or are they *human doings*?

To be fair, there are other ways we establish value, but the quickest one is to measure people's value based on some combination of *what they do* and *who they are*. The "what they do" category is the easiest to quantify, and we tend to use that first. Think of a typical conversation between two men who have just been introduced to each other. "Jim, this is Bob. Bob, this is Jim." We all know what comes next. Jim says something like, "Good to meet you, Bob. *So, what do you do?*" If Bob has the kind of job that Jim feels comfortable with—if it puts him into a social stratum that's close to his—then he feels like he can relate to him. If he's too far above or below his spot on the social or economic pecking order, the conversation concludes with a polite, "Well, nice to meet you, Bob," and Jim moves on. What Jim has done is make two value judgments—one about Bob and one about himself. We probably recognize that it's hopelessly inaccurate to make those kinds of value judgments about others that quickly, but it's all we've got to go on at first. That we make them so quickly about ourselves is also unfortunate—it reflects how poorly most of us actually know ourselves.

Understanding the difference between doing and being can change how we see the world around us.

Measuring people's value based on what they do is not necessarily wrong. Nor is measuring their value by what they do for us necessarily selfish. For example, recommending the contractor who did a home renovation is based on what he *did*. He might not have been good at conversation, but we didn't hire him to talk to us. He might not have been a very good husband or father, but as long as he's good at carpentry, he'll get the recommendation. We might even place high value on people who aren't particularly likable, if they help get a job done. For example, there are things we would not have learned if not forced to do so by someone, but because we're not usually appreciative of their "help" at the time, we can hardly be accused of being selfish!

The much more complex option for establishing a person's value is to base it on *who they are*. One of the things we like to do in our seminars, particularly when the audience is composed primarily of men, is to say, "Write down one paragraph that explains *who you are*, without saying anything about *what you do*. You can't write 'I'm a manager' or 'I'm a teacher.' Those things are what you *do*. You have to stick to telling us who you *are*." The room dissolves into puzzled looks, as people who have defined almost everything about themselves by what they do and how they perform try to figure out what to write. (Women can usually write one sentence, although they can't usually get too much farther than that. North American culture seems to allow women to establish their value in things that are concerned with *being* than with *doing* more than it allows men the same privilege.) Why don't you try the exercise? Take a few minutes and think about it. What would you write?

Are you a business manager, trying to generate enough income to pay off a mortgage and sock away enough cash to help your daughter through college? Or are you a careful planner who works hard on keeping a balance between work and home, between being a good provider and a best friend for your teenager, and you worry that you're not getting it quite right?

Are you "just a salesperson," or are you someone who really enjoys meeting new people and loves to spend time figuring out how you can help them with products or services that you believe in and are excited about sharing with them?

Understanding the difference between *doing* and *being* can change how we see the world around us. Is the young lady who served you lunch in the restaurant "just a waitress," or is she a diligent young woman, working her way through college, following her dream to bring a better life to underprivileged people? And here's the *real* question: Will she be a *different person* when she's not working at the restaurant anymore and gets a position as a partner in the local law firm? Of course not! And, while it's likely that she's going to generate a bigger *salary* at the law firm, does she have more *value*?

It doesn't take long to discover that we don't know very much about establishing a person's value based on who they are. Most of the time, we *simply don't know* who they are and don't have the time or energy to invest in the level of relationship that it takes to find out. Who we are is a combination of preferences, beliefs, values, defense mechanisms, insecurities, and a lot of other stuff. It's a complicated potpourri of variables that would take a lot of work to describe fully. (Later in the book, in Sections 2 and 3, we're going to give you lots of thoughts on how to measure people's value. For now, we want to focus specifically on the definition rather than on its application.)

The Left Ditch – The Slave Driver

If our normal measurement of people's value is based on what they do, there's a flaw in the foundation of our values. When the pressure builds up, the dam will burst. Why? Because it's inevitable that people will disappoint us. Eventually everyone we know is going to do something that we'd rather they wouldn't have! Ironically, it's a fact of relationships that those who are closest to us and we trust the most also have the greatest capacity to hurt us—and they do. All of us have said something that we wish we could take back; we've all done something that we realized later was a mistake. And if our internal measurement system only evaluates what people *do* as a measure of their value, every time they disappoint us, we subconsciously take a couple of points off their worth. We start treating them as though we don't value them as much. Eventually, we treat them as though they're worthless. This leads to the left ditch slave driver mindset which is fundamentally to use people up for as much production value as they can provide and then discard them.

There's another subtle flaw in that measurement system. Ancient wisdom says, "Those who live by the sword, die by the sword." People who determine the value of others based on what they do probably base their own self-worth on what they do. When they live up to their own expectations, they feel good about themselves. When they fall short, they struggle with self-esteem. If they really blow it, they think of themselves as worthless.

The problem with a value system in the left-ditch that sets the worth of a person based exclusively on what they do is that very few people want it applied to *them*. We don't want to be thought of as less valuable just because we've made a mistake, can't work as quickly as someone else, or (heaven forbid) get too old or sick to work anymore. Some would like us to believe that value is a relativistic measurement that's tied to our usefulness to society. The more useful we are, the more we're worth. But, if we're not seen as useful, then we're close to worthless.

What does that look like in the real world? In Edmonton, Alberta, where we have an office, there's been an ongoing investigation for years into sex-trade workers disappearing and then being found murdered in farmer's fields around the city. It is remarkable how many people seem to have the attitude that these are "just prostitutes," as though somehow they aren't worth the effort of tracking down those responsible. We don't want to suggest that there's a lack of resolve on the part of the authorities in trying to solve these crimes—they're working as diligently as they can. We're talking about the attitude of the people who read the newspapers and watch the news. It makes us wonder: if these were teachers or bank tellers that were being found dead, would there suddenly be a lot more public pressure to track down the person or persons who are responsible? Surely these women still have value *for who they are*, even though we might have strong feelings about *what they do*?

The Right Ditch – The People Pleaser

There is an opposite position on the right edge of the road. Instead of treating people primarily for their economic value, the focus of a businesses' human resources policy would need to lean exclusively toward the needs and wants of employees. The organization would become overly concerned with pleasing staff, even at the expense of customers and productivity. A business wouldn't survive very long if it operated at this extreme.

There are plenty of people who demonstrate by their comments and opinions that they think a business *should* run at this opposite extreme. In our seminars, it's unusual to have an audience that doesn't include at least a handful of people who feel that failure to put the needs of employees at such a high priority is unethical, even immoral. It may well be that some of these folks are trying to push the pendulum far to the right side, hoping that it will settle somewhere near the middle. At the same time, it's easy to see how any attempt to evaluate others can quickly become a system for ranking people according to their value. And, in the minds of many people, trying to claim that one person is worth more than another (or conversely that one person is worth *less* than another) is inappropriate.

The challenge at the right extreme is in trying to believe that somehow, saying people have value only outside of what they do means that everyone has exactly the *same value*. If that's true, then there's no justification for paying different salaries to people who handle varying levels of responsibility and solve problems of differing complexity.

Value-Related Pain Points

When the workplace treats employees without balance in the area of the employee's intrinsic value there are a lot of unhealthy symptoms—these result in poor organizational health. We've identified 7 warning signs that organizational dysfunction rooted values-related thinking exist.

1. Reluctance to do anything extra

Employees "work to rule" more often. They do precisely what's asked of them, whether they know more effective ways or not. They want to

21

be paid for every bit of effort they expend. We hear things like, "They don't pay me to think." Employees who don't feel valued by their employer don't have any incentive to add value; people who feel abused become abusive.

2. Decreased productivity

Decreased productivity and low motivation are common. Why work hard for somebody who doesn't care anyway? Have you ever heard anyone say, "Don't ask me! I just work here."? If people feel that the value they've tried to add isn't appreciated or wanted, they stop trying to add it.

3. Unethical behavior and absenteeism

Unethical behavior is easily justified by staff members who feel undervalued. "They don't pay me what I'm worth, so I don't have a problem helping myself to make up for it." That not only applies to petty theft, such as stationery and tools, it also applies to time. Employees punch in before they even take off their coats, pause to read the morning paper, and have their first cup of coffee before they start to work. Absenteeism is significantly higher in organizations where there is value-related dysfunction. Because loyalty is lower, the slightest excuse will do for nonattendance.

4. Increased conflict and unrest

Conflict and unrest are much higher when staff members don't feel that the organization values them. Even the best intentions on the part of the company receive a negative interpretation. Because the environment seems negative, people tend to look out for their own interests ahead of the interests of others. Suspicion about wrong motives and hidden agendas become the norm. When the only reflection of perceived value is through positions and perks, unhealthy competition and jealousy make every promotion or organizational change a potential battlefield.

5. Lack of commitment

Employees who feel undervalued engage in undue worry—about their job security, the organization's health and how that will affect them, the motives of their supervisors and peers, and just about anything else that they don't understand. Because they feel that the company isn't really committed to them, they feel justified in their lack of commitment to the company.

6. Leaders are unwilling to make tough decisions

Because leaders don't want to hurt anybody, they waffle, are indecisive, or make decisions and then reverse them. Sometimes, rather than work through issues with people who are resisting them, leaders just change directions abruptly. In the process, they sideline the people who used to be "in their way." Instead of working through the challenges of building a strong cohesive team, they try to make decisions that will be popular or easy for their employees to accept. The false hope is that this will somehow reduce conflict.

7. Letting issues slide, hoping they will go away.

So that they don't appear to be undervaluing anyone, leaders put off making hard personnel decisions hoping that things will somehow resolve themselves. They hope that, given a little more time, the person will correct their own divisive or abusive behavior.

Abusive or divisive people are often high performers. When confronted with their behavior, they hide behind their ability to produce. Ironically, when leaders won't deal with employees who behave badly, others on the team feel devalued.

Why does it matter?

What employers and businesses have lost when they don't clearly communicate value to employees is the cooperation of staff in identifying and solving business problems and capitalizing on opportunities.

When people feel wrongly valued, they automatically move to a win-lose perspective: to allow the employer to win any sort of concession is seen as validating or endorsing the inappropriate methods of valuation and is therefore seen as a loss for the employee. To win, and assert their *real* value, employees have to force the employer to lose and give up ground.

Case Study

Kim is a hardworking mother of four who has reached the upper end of her career as a nurse. She's a smart, humble, and valuable employee. The senior person on duty in an important emergency medical facility, hard work and dedication has paid off for her. For years she'd loved work and felt that she was making a difference. Her work was tiring but satisfying, and her future looked great.

As Kim's family grew, vacations became more important to her. She put in a request for two weeks off, but her manager reminded Kim that she was the only one with specific levels of certifications and two weeks off just wasn't feasible. "How about three days?" At first, Kim was willing to see her manager's point. However, junior staff were being granted contiguous weeks off on a regular basis. Her manager's reply was, "Kim, they can't do what you can, and we need you!"

For two years, Kim made requests for time off and was consistently met with resistance. It wasn't so much the excuses that were bothering her; it was something she couldn't quite describe. She felt like a piece of machinery, not a human. She started to take sick days to deal with stress. Her work ethic made her feel guilty for staying home, but she needed the chance to get away and rest. She had lost the will to out-give her employer.

In her heart, Kim knew something was wrong. She couldn't live in agreement with a way of being valued that was not sustainable long term. Her friends told her, "Stick it out. You can't find a reasonable manager in this industry." In what seemed like a high risk, poorly planned decision, Kim quit. She gave up her tenure, pension, benefits, and all the guarantees the union and her hospital had to offer. She took a position with a private start-up. No guarantees, lower pay, few benefits, and only the hope for a pension someday.

Kim tells the story like it happened yesterday. She'd been at her new job three months. The doctor at the new clinic, her boss, passed Kim in the hall. As their eyes met to greet each another, the doctor stopped to ask if everything was okay. Kim assured him it was nothing. The doctor pressed her, and Kim let him know that her daughter had just called from school: she was sick and throwing up. Kim had arranged for her daughter to rest in the office at the school so she could finish her appointments and take a break. She apologized for bothering him with her messy life. What the doctor did next took her by complete surprise: he told her to go immediately and be with her daughter. At first, Kim protested, assuming that this would be held against her, yet something told her this time it wouldn't be. Her boss took care of her last appointment that morning and then personally contacted the afternoon clients to rebook their appointments. He also took a minute to let her know that he was more than glad to give her any additional support she might need that day. She felt so valued and so important. In a moment, the doctor had established Kim's worth in a way she had not thought possible at work

Kim has shared the story over and over, adding proudly that she's worked countless overtime hours and has gone the extra mile for her doctor in the four years that have followed. She's only had one sick day in the whole time. She is very clear on one thing: "Just treat me like a human, grant me a break when I need it, and I'll pay it back ten if not twenty times over."

Actually, Kim's math is off a bit. When we interviewed her, we took a minute to do the calculation. She figures she's worked a minimum ten extra hours a month since that event with no charge to the doctor. That means he's received 480 hours in return for a four-hour investment: that would be 120 times over. Kim says she'll never go back to her previous employer or anyone else who to treats her as a human doing, not a human being.

Questions

Can you think of times when you've felt like Kim did with her first employer? When staff come to you with a request, is your first reaction to say "No", or do you listen carefully to the request and see how you can work it through? What lesson can be learned from the fact that it took two questions from Kim's second boss before she dared to share what was bothering her?

As you reflect on Kim's story, consider your own leadership style: are you more like her first boss or her second one? What are the steps you can take in your organization to begin treating people more like *human beings* than like *human doings*?

The Road of Balance

People who believe they are seen as valuable not only for what they do but also for *who they are* tend to be happier and more engaged than those who believe they are seen purely for their ability to produce. The end result is a win-win:

> ➢ Employees create less conflict in their work environment, getting along with each other more easily, cooperating with leadership more readily, and buying in to solutions with more than just lip service.

> ➢ Staff members are willing to take reasonable risks and share the load when extra effort is needed, without feeling as though their cooperation is likely to be abused or taken for granted.

> ➢ Turnover is lower—people are more satisfied with their jobs, even when working conditions aren't ideal. They're willing to accept less than ideal surroundings, because they feel that they

themselves are valued and stop assuming that the work environment is the only reflection of their employer's appreciation for them.

➤ People who see themselves as valued are more loyal. They're more willing to trust decisions made by leaders and feel less compelled to complain when things don't go as planned. When they see themselves as valued, they assume that decisions are being made with their interests at heart.

➤ Staff members are more creative in the work that they do. Because they have higher job satisfaction, they're willing to invest creative energy more freely. And, because they feel valued, they're less concerned about whether or not they are "compensated" for their creativity.

➤ They are confident, because they are valued, that they will be part of the organization for the long term. That makes them more willing to put in the effort to resolve conflict and invest in building relationships.

➤ They treat misunderstanding with a positive interpretation. Staff members are more likely to say, "I'm sure that was a mistake; it's not like them to treat me that way."

Summary

Employees who work under a balanced system for this value add the creativity that's needed to "make the difference" in terms of quality, efficiency, and customer service. They contribute to process improvement because they feel that they are stakeholders in the outcome.

We introduced the value system with a question, "What are people worth?" But there's a principle behind the question that identifies the nature of a balanced position: *People have inherent value that goes beyond their ability to produce or to please.* Organizations understanding this find ways to let people know that they're appreciated, indicating that it's the people who matter, not just the bottom line.

In many ways, the remaining principles are an expression of this first one. Genuinely believing that people have intrinsic value allows the remaining principles to become the expression of that value. This first principle is foundational. Without it, following the others will seem patronizing or manipulative—a way to try and wring a little more productivity from an unwilling workforce.

How do we view people's value? Does our assessment go deeper than pure economic or utilitarian measurement? How do we view our own value? Is our self-esteem based on how well we scored in the latest evaluation, or do we recognize that our value lies in far deeper and more abstract qualities?

Chapter 3: Aptitude

Recognizing Gifts and Talents

How do you see your leadership role? Do you prefer to assign tasks and focus on getting the job done, or do you see your role as recognizing, cultivating, and developing gifts and abilities in others?

Every person has gifts and abilities of some kind. Some of those gifts are well developed; some are still latent and waiting to be discovered. Aptitude refers to the way we respond to those gifts and abilities.

For Aptitude, the ditch on the left side of the road is labeled Just Get It Done. People living at that extreme have a highly directive point of view, seeing employees as simply contractors—people hired to do a job, without any investment in a long-term relationship. Workers are treated based on their present skills and abilities, without any regard for their personal needs or aspirations. To these leaders, supervision means get the job done.

Gifts and abilities are essential parts of who a person is and what they were destined to do.

We label the ditch on the right side of the road the Soft Touch. Leaders who think and live with this perspective become enablers in an unhealthy, permissive relationship that virtually smothers the employee. Meeting the personal needs and aspirations of workers is primary, whether it makes economic sense or not.

Just Get It Done (Directive)	Balanced	Soft Touch (Permissive)
• Disregard the importance of people's gifts. • Ignoring gifts when assigning tasks. • If you don't meet the standards or the targets, you'll be replaced.	• Gifts and abilities are considered in recruiting and selecting. • Help employees discover their gifts. • Match gifts to the right area of responsibility. • Hold staff accountable for excellent performance.	• Spend too much time tailoring assignments. • Work isn't done if someone doesn't like doing it. • Permit poor performance in out-of-gift areas.

In the corporate setting, if things come together the way they should, the people who are put into a particular job or role will have a gift that gives them that natural edge, such as the salesman who has an unbelievable knack for knowing just what to say and when to say it or the customer service agent who has a talent for soothing an irritable client. When we get it right, it works well. Unfortunately, we know it doesn't always come together that easily. There are times when the job just has to get done, and whether someone's particularly gifted or not, we need them to buckle down and do it.

The Left Ditch – Just Get It Done

At the left extreme, we completely disregard the whole concept of gifts and abilities. Gifts and abilities and likes and dislikes all become irrelevant. "You were hired to do a job, and if you won't do it, then we need to replace you with someone who will." It's not the employer's responsibility to make an employee feel happy. The supervisor's job is to crack the whip and deliver, not to cater to the whims of staff.

In the real world, the left-ditch perspective isn't usually quite that extreme. What we do see is the sentiment that a business has to make money in order to keep the doors open. If the staff don't produce, it's not a question of whether people *like* their jobs; it's a question of whether they *have them*. If we move staff members around, it costs money to train them for a new job and to train others to take the ones they've moved out of. Employees are productive with the job they know and won't be productive right away in a new one; the same goes for their replacements. In some ways it's like the old saying, "Rather the devil you know than the devil you don't." Furthermore, there are things that have to be done that nobody particularly likes. "Sometimes, you've got to do what you've got to do." We could sum this perspective up by saying, "Your job is your *job*, not your *life*. If you don't feel fulfilled, then find something that's enjoyable outside of work and be fulfilled in that."

It's amazing how many organizations actually live near the left edge on this value system. There's quite a bit of dysfunction and organizational pain that finds its roots on the left side of Aptitude-related thinking.

Consider front-line service people. They are told that they are expected to deal with customers in a courteous and professional manner; that they are there to "serve" the customers (hence the term "service" in their job title). But who do they *really* serve—the customers or the supervisors who hold them accountable and do their evaluations? We'd like to think the answer is the customers, but we know that in a lot of cases, the real answer is the supervisors. But don't blame the supervisors. Who do the supervisors actually serve: managers or the front-line staff who are supposedly serving the customers? And it carries right up the chain of command. How does a frustrated customer get some kind of satisfaction? Simple—go above the head of the front-line staff, and get a manager involved! That way, the supervisor will tell the line staff that the manager has authorized them to do something that is contrary to policy. And, because the supervisor *told* them to do it that way, they know they won't get in trouble for it.

When recruiting a customer service representative, companies go to great lengths to find someone who scores well on people skills, problem resolution skills, and the ability to diffuse conflict and find a win-win. They want people with natural gifts in those areas to deal with customers. But where are those gifts and skills are actually getting used, if they're getting used at all? Are supervisors giving staff the opportunity to use those gifts and skills to keep customers happy, or are they much more concerned about enforcing policy? Are they allowing staff to focus on actually *solving* problems, or are they much more concerned about simply making the problems *disappear*?

The Right Ditch – Soft Touch

At the other end of this extreme, we would spend all our time trying to make sure that we tailor every assignment to the preferences, likes, and dislikes of our employees. We don't want to ruffle any feathers. If we can't find someone who likes the job, it just doesn't get done or we do it ourselves. If someone gets tired of the job they do, we have to work at helping them figure out what they *do* like and then find them a new task that suits their new preference. We shudder at confrontation and hate dealing with poor performance—we don't want to make anyone feel threatened.

Buried in the right-ditch position there is a sense that people have the *right* to independence and free-thinking. If they feel that there are better ways to do their jobs, they have the right to give it a try. The people who live closest to the problems are often the ones who have the best perspective on how to solve them. If the focus on empowering people to innovate results in a loss of productivity, we're hesitant to confront people or hold them accountable—after all, we don't want to limit their creativity. At this end of the scale, conflict is seen as being bad and to be avoided at any cost. Maybe they'll do better next time. Maybe they're just "going through something," and if we give them a little space, they'll improve.

Obviously, neither of the extremes is a particularly healthy position. If we ignore people's preferences, we're either going to have an unmanageable turnover problem or a major productivity problem. If we refuse to deal with difficult situations, we get a similar problem— we may not have the turnover, but we still get no output! Either way, the company ends up laying everyone off when it goes bankrupt.

Here is a symptom of an organization that lives near the right extreme. Have you ever called a supplier to talk about some kind of mistake they've made and been treated cordially and respectfully, only to have the mistake repeated the next time you deal with them? You call, and they're really helpful about solving the problem, but the mistake is repeated a third time?

On the left extreme, people aren't allowed to use their gifts and skills because they're too busy trying to live within the constraints imposed by culture and policy. But on the right extreme, there is virtually no accountability for mistakes and very little in the way of process that helps assure errors won't be repeated. The focus on allowing people to use their gifts has gone to the point where correction and accountability don't exist. To the customer, this can be exasperating! Even though the service staff is courteous and professional, the mistake won't go away! It gets repeated over and over.

Aptitude-Related Pain Points

We've identified six practical signs that organizational dysfunction, rooted in misunderstanding how to apply people's gifts properly, has set in.

1. Loss of productivity

A consistent downward trend in per person productivity can be an indicator that dysfunction is festering below the surface. Increased costs due to waste or rework can indicate that people are finding it difficult to stay excited about what they're doing. The people who are the highest producers are the ones who are doing what they *love* to do.

2. Lack of innovation

People who are working "in the zone"—in an area where they have aptitude—are much more innovative than those who are "just putting in time." A reduction in organizational learning and growth—people don't seem to care about finding better ways to do things—is a strong indicator that there are problems under the surface. People who are working in ways that play to their strengths are naturally more innovative than those who are working where they don't have natural, intuitive ability.

3. Low staff commitment

People who are working in areas where they have natural gifts say things like, "I'd do this job even if they didn't pay me!" That's probably an exaggeration on their part, but it indicates a high level of commitment to the organization. On the other hand, we've all heard people say, "You couldn't pay me enough to do *that* job." Realistically, we could probably pay them enough to get them to do it for a while, but eventually pay alone is not a good enough motivator to keep people committed. Real commitment comes when people see the value in what they do, and thoroughly enjoy doing it.

4. Low trust levels

Low trust levels lead to slow decision making and a lot of speculation and suspicion about hidden agendas, which is very detrimental to the future success of the organization. Organizations that have high levels of trust avoid the lost time associated with endless meetings to explain motives, threats by employees to thwart change, and unofficial "work to rule" campaigns by people who refuse to do anything beyond what's in their job description. Trust is high in organizations where people believe that their personal interests are being considered.

5. Lack of focus/engagement

When employees aren't working in a gift area they tend to lack focus. Because their interest isn't fully engaged they start focusing in directions more in keeping with their natural gifts, than the corporate direction the job requires. Even though the employee shows up for work they're not fully engaged in the job.

6. High staff turnover

People who aren't happy with their jobs eventually leave them. High turnover has some pretty serious ramifications for an organization— for one thing, it's terribly expensive. Training costs go up, productivity stays low because there are so many new people, and experienced staff gets sidetracked by all the training they have to do. (If experienced staff doesn't like doing the training, their job satisfaction goes down, and the problem gets exponentially worse.)

7. Soft injury and disability

People who find that they need to force themselves to go to work are more likely to experience stress and depression because of the work environment, something human resources professionals call "soft injury." Stress leave and clinical depression are expensive for the organization, and they create pressure at home for the employee to find new, more satisfying, less stressful employment.

Why does it matter?

What about the argument that says, "We've gotten this far and been successful. Why change?" Obviously, no one *has* to change. Determining the point at which the paradox is balanced is up to each organization and leader. We believe that bringing *social considerations* back to the table is important for long-term workplace health. Economic drivers without a commitment to considering people's gifts and abilities lead to negative results and organizations that slowly succumb to organizational dysfunction. A fit, healthy body resists disease more effectively than an unfit one does. Our hope is that organizations will see the value in making sure that there's a healthy balance between the task-oriented, business-economic drivers for decisions and the people-oriented, social considerations that will ensure ongoing organizational health.

The Road of Balance

There are a few guidelines that help define the middle ground and when we're getting off toward an extreme.

First, all other things being equal (which they normally aren't), it's better to give assignments to people who enjoy doing the jobs than to give them to people who don't. Unless an assignment is short term, it's not likely that employees will stick around long if they're consistently given assignments they dislike. People are more likely to focus on quality if they like the jobs they do, and they're more likely to accept poor quality if they don't. Assigning jobs to people who simply *don't like doing them* is *the* proverbial "accident waiting for a chance to happen" scenario. At the same time, it isn't hard to find examples where people *thought* they weren't going to like an assignment but then discovered that over time, they became very good at the jobs and enjoyed them. There are also times when a leader's foresight tells them that even though a person *thinks* they'll like the job, they're not going to find it very fulfilling.

Second, we don't have a responsibility to make people happy. Happiness isn't directly related to circumstance. It's a much more holistic measure of the entire scope of a person's life. It's unrealistic to assume that out of the 168 hours in every week, 40 of them can make it or break it in terms of happiness—it's not as though the other 128 don't count! At the same time, because we sleep for around 50 of those hours, work time amounts to roughly one-third of our waking hours. So, while it's not an employer's responsibility to keep people feeling happy, it sure makes life more enjoyable when people like what they do at work!

Third, we actually have a *responsibility* to guide and correct staff when they do work that falls below expectations. That statement might be a bit surprising, because it's much easier to ignore problems than to confront them and correct them. But, correction doesn't have to be harsh to be effective, and giving no correction at all can be just as abusive as being merciless. Refusing to correct someone can be equivalent to saying, "I don't care about you; I'm not interested enough in you to bother helping you improve." Managers and supervisors in an organization have the unique responsibility of assigning staff the tasks that have to be done, in a way that maximizes the benefit to the company, staff, *and* clients or customers.

So how do we do the balancing act for this value? How do we find the place where we can get the job done and leave enough freedom to allow people to feel like they have some room to breathe and innovate?

Case Study

Sarah was a bright young lady who came into one of our client's offices in an entry-level position. Six months after she started, she got a competing offer and showed up to ask for a raise or a promotion; otherwise she was leaving. Her employer is committed to maintaining a healthy organization and was willing to put in the effort to make sure Sarah would be happy. They spent a few minutes with Sarah, helping her think through some insightful questions.

Sarah discovered that what she loved best about her job was the opportunity to do lots of different creative things as part of her day. As the receptionist for a busy professional office, she had a steady flow of people asking her for help with all kinds of projects. It didn't take long for Sarah to realize that the new opportunity, enticing because it was for more money, would never offer her the opportunity to be creative, solve problems, or interact with lots of interesting people. She stayed—a win-win solution. Our client retained the investment in Sarah's training and experience, and Sarah found a way to be happy with her job again.

In a less healthy organization, Sarah might have been told, "We just don't have a different position for you, and we really can't justify giving you a raise at this point in time. There's really nothing we can do for you." They would have lost a really good receptionist, and in the end, Sarah wouldn't have been happy either. We can think, "That's just the way it goes sometimes." But it would have been a lose-lose situation.

The difference between a healthy organization and an unhealthy one can be subtle. In Sarah's case, the difference between our client and a less healthy organization that would have let her walk away was probably less than half an hour! The much bigger difference is that our client has committed to a policy of always considering what would be best for each employee in every decision. They've found a way to balance the equation that seems to give them happy employees *and* good returns on their investments.

Questions

Think back to the last time someone left your team or organization— did you take the time to sit down with them and discover why they were leaving, with the motive of doing your best to keep them? Do you view staff as *fish*—there are always more where that one came from, or as *stars*—each one shines brightly when placed in the right position and given the right support?

It takes time to know your people, and what they are good at. What three things can you do in the next three months to gain a better understanding of the people in your team or organization?

The Leader's Role

Later in the book, in Sections 2 and 3, we're going to dig into the question of how to measure aptitude and apply a balanced perspective to the value. For now, we want to focus specifically on the definition, rather than on its application.

In a healthy organization, leaders understand that they serve the people who report to them. A leader's job is to ensure that the team has the resources, direction, training, and empowerment to do the job that it needs to do. Leaders understand that the team is not there to serve them—they are there to serve the team. At the same time, leaders aren't afraid to deal objectively with issues. If staff members aren't doing a good job of serving their teams or customers, leaders aren't hesitant about correcting wrong attitudes or behaviors. In fact, part of *serving* includes holding people accountable for meeting standards and achieving performance targets.

If an organization expects front-line staff to find creative ways to make sure that customers have their needs met, are happy with the products or services, and keep coming back for more, then they need to apply that same logic all the way up the structure. In a healthy organization, leaders accept responsibility to understand the gifts, aptitudes, and preferences of those they lead. They ensure that people fit properly into the organization, in keeping with their gifts and abilities. They find ways to play to their strengths and support them where they're weak. Leaders also accept responsibility to ensure that the organization is economically healthy. They ensure that people are productive and contributing to the overall picture.

What do we do when people aren't happy or aren't feeling good about the job they have to do, and there aren't other opportunities available for them? Ideally, we do what our client did for Sarah— find new ways to inspire them and keep them motivated. But, there are times when doing the right thing means helping them find a new position *outside* of the team, department, or even the organization, because there isn't a way for them to be fully fulfilled inside it. If we're committed to helping people develop their gifts and abilities, and we're convinced that we want people to work in jobs where their gifts and abilities fit the requirements of the job, then we're obliged to help people find such a position—even if it means we help them find a new job working for someone else.

Leadership gurus Robert K. Greenleaf, Warren G. Bennis, Ken Blanchard,[4] and others have written about a concept called servant leadership. Servant leadership recognizes that leaders make a number of unique contributions to their teams. There are five things that they must focus their time and effort on:

1. **Vision:** The team can't run off on its own, doing whatever each team member feels like doing. Following more than one vision at a time is unhealthy and impractical. Two visions equal di**vision**. One of the most important jobs leaders do is keep team members focused on the vision—why they are there, how their input helps the organization, and what they can do to help the organization improve.

2. **Training:** Leaders are there to make sure team members know how to do their jobs effectively. They don't necessarily have to do the training themselves, but they do have to recognize when and where training is necessary and make sure that the necessary training is properly facilitated in terms of schedules and resources.

3. **Authority:** Leader have the right to use authority (wisely, of course) to settle matters of disagreement, questions of direction or method, and so on. Leaders who won't exercise authority when it's appropriate to do so essentially abdicate the role of leader.

4. **Resources:** Leaders have access to resources that team members do not, and may not even be aware of. They can negotiate with other departments or other leaders for staff, budget, equipment, etc. far more effectively than team members can.

5. **Accountability:** Leaders, have the right to hold team members accountable for their performance. Accountability isn't equivalent to dictatorship! Accountability means that leaders have the right to ask for an accounting of how the team as a whole, and the team members as individuals, are spending time and resources to produce what the team is expected to contribute.

Essentially, in the servant leadership model, supervisors and leaders are there to do whatever the team *cannot* do for themselves—and *only* what the team cannot do for themselves. Leading isn't about being the "boss"; it's about helping people do their jobs well.

Organizations can live out a balanced position on Aptitude in a number of practical ways:

➤ Hire new employees based on a broader set of criteria than skill, education, and experience. Choose people who will fit in to the organization and be the most productive. Hire those who will fit in to the culture and bring strengths to the job, instead of hiring those who have the skills and experience but don't measure up in terms of character. Factor in questions of character and giftedness up front.

Get acquainted with some form of character-based testing for staff, like Myers-Briggs, DISC, and our WRI tool (see Chapter 10) and launch a process to get everyone to complete the profiles. Leaders need to know the people who work for them! Put together a list of the gifts that each position requires and start thinking about who fits where. It will start to pay dividends when leaders can say, "I think Susan would do really well in sales. She has this gift and that gift, which are key requirements for a successful salesperson. Let's talk to her about joining the sales team."

> Reengineer the entire hiring process so that it helps employees already in the organization to find their "right place," before hiring from outside to fill a vacancy. Become proactive about finding ways to redeploy employees who are struggling in their present position. And, don't hesitate to recommend that an employee seek employment elsewhere if that's the *right thing* to do in the specific situation.

> Create professional development strategies that encourage and reward growth and development beyond demonstrable job skills. Encourage people to take courses that help them on a much broader scale than what their job might require on the surface. For example, some of our clients subsidize marriage enrichment or parenting skill seminars for any employee—less stress at home equals better productivity on the job. Seminars on managing personal investments, open for family members, are usually well-attended. When an employer's motives are clear, reaching beyond the workplace into the home like that builds tremendous loyalty with employees and their families.

> Consider developing an apprenticeship program that's designed to give inexperienced or under-qualified employment candidates an opportunity to learn the job at reduced wages. It may be a way to hire people who have the right character and gifts, even though they don't have the skills and experience. Adding an incentive pay program to encourage and reward those who make good progress helps identify the people who have the self-discipline to make great employees!

Before this starts to sound too easy, take five minutes and write down some of your own unique talents and abilities. Then, write down some of the unique talents and abilities of people you work fairly closely with. Now, jot down two or three things that you have to do that really aren't pleasant for you, especially if you're not gifted in that area. Then, do the same thing for those you work closely with. Is there an opportunity to reorganize some responsibilities? Are you gifted at something someone else has to do but isn't gifted at? Can you move toward reassigning some of your less pleasant responsibilities to someone who would consider them a treat?

Summary

Leaders who understand the process of looking at the gifts and aptitudes of the people they lead bring a value of their own to their organizations. They motivate and coach people into situations where they're ideally suited to do the jobs they do. The key to success in this area is having clear, obvious motives that are focused on helping others. If leaders' motives are primarily focused on bolstering their own chances for success, their motives will betray them—staff will quickly see through what is happening and see the process as "using them" to accomplish a selfish goal. On the other hand, when leaders genuinely believe that their own success is wrapped up in the success of those they lead, organizational health is not far behind.

Employees who work under a balanced system work from a sense of being "rightly placed" and are deeply motivated to do well, now that they are in the vocation that best suits their gifts and abilities. They have confidence that, if they need to be corrected, supervisors will treat them with dignity, honesty and respect. (Leaders can't be so soft that they're unwilling to challenge people to produce at levels that are in keeping with their gifts.)

It's important to add that to be truly effective as leaders, supervisors and managers must be able to get some of their own sense of accomplishment vicariously. In other words, they have to be able to achieve fulfillment through the work of others, rather than through their own effort. Supervisors who aren't objective about their own gifts and abilities tend to limit the degree to which they empower and enable their teams to do what they themselves cannot do. One high-performing leader put it this way, "I'm not here to try and get you to help *me* reach *my* goals; I'm here to help *you* reach *your* goals—that *is* my goal!"

Chapter 4: Learning

Promoting Personal Development and Growth

People want to learn new things, to feel they've made a contribu-tion—that they are doing worthwhile work. Few people are moti-vated only by money. People want to feel that what they do makes a difference in the world.

—*Frances Hesselbien, President, Peter F. Drucker Foundation*

In leadership, how do you see your role as a mentor or coach? Do you see yourself as primarily a job-skills coach who doesn't get involved with employee's "personality issues?" Or, do you have a responsibility to help the people you lead grow in a much broader sense?

The ditch on the left side of the road of learning is called On Your Own Dime, an attitude of indifference toward learning and growth. If employees don't have the character qualities to handle the job, the organization either ignores that fact and muddles ahead or rep-laces them with people who do. They think, "We're not in the business of developing people; we're in the busi-ness of building or selling products or services."

> **People need to grow if they are to experience success.**

The ditch on the right side of the road is manipulation, and it's called We Know What's Best for You. Because companies presume that certain charac-ter qualities are necessary, they do everything they can to force people to act as though they have exactly those qualities. They use intimidation, shame, blame, and any other weapon they can find to try and force employees to live up to their expectations.

On Your Own Dime (Indifference)	Balanced	We Know What's Best for You (Manipulation)
• Why invest in others if they already do what you need them to? • Protectionism: no one else can learn to do this job; withhold information to keep an "edge". • Training is tightly controlled by supervisors.	• We believe in you and want you to grow; leaders are catalysts in employee growth. • Provide the supportive environment for mentoring to occur. • Communicate openly and honestly, especially with bad news. • Discipline is restorative, not punitive.	• People must take growth training prescribed. • Patronizing attitudes and words are common. • No one gets promoted without an assigned mentor.

By nature, people want to grow. If your home is typical of homes with growing children, there is a section of wall that has been used over the years to mark the height of each child as they grew. It's almost as if there is a contest to see who can grow more. There's something about that little mark on the wall that *proves* that there's progress over time.

We see the effects of this innate desire to grow all around us. People want to improve their standard of living, absorb information, and many want promotion and growth in their careers. (Even in a corrupt community—among thieves or other criminals, for example—people want to grow; there will be a natural competition to see who can be the best thief or criminal.)

There are lots of areas where we grow as we learn new things, but the one that we want to focus on primarily is character development. It's good when people grow in terms of skills or abilities, but isn't that more or less expected of employees? We expect people to improve as they gain experience, and it would be rare to find an employee who thought that was unreasonable. But mention character development and see if that doesn't create a raised eyebrow or two! We've heard things like, "Listen, you can tell me how to work, but you can't tell me how to live!" and, "You don't own me! You can't tell me what kind of a person to be!" It's almost as though there is a disconnect between who a person is at work and who they are everywhere else.

> "The process of personal growth is an effortful and difficult one. This is because it is conducted against a natural resistance, against a natural inclination to keep things the way they were, to cling to the old maps and old ways of doing things, to take the easy path."
>
> —M. Scott Peck,
> The Road Less Traveled

But let's face it: who people are outside of work *does* affect who they are at work. If employees are going through difficult times, such as disagreeing with a spouse or a child, or if they're under financial pressure or struggling with other personal issues, that stress finds its way back to the office or the jobsite. And, if there are character flaws that are either causing or adding to those situations, those same character flaws are going to create or exacerbate problems at work too.

So, why do people seem to resist growth in terms of their character? Perhaps because they've failed so many times that they've given up. "Why bother trying? This is the way I am, and there's nothing I can do about it." Or maybe it's because they simply don't realize that they have an issue. It's in their blind spot, and they're simply unaware that their own character flaws are the source of the issues that seem to follow them wherever they go.

Self-motivated character growth is good, but it's relatively rare. There are plenty of people who set sales, career, earning, and vacation goals for themselves. Most of the time though, it seems that goals related to character growth are set by others—they come through a relationship with someone who *does* see the problem clearly and can give the insight and feedback that's necessary—a mentor or a coach of some sort. It's the feedback from the coach or mentor that eventually creates character change. Over time, pointing out troublesome patterns of thinking or reacting helps people become more sensitive and deal with the issues. It could also come from a spouse or close friend, an employer, or even a valued employee. A more sensitive person will pick up on the cues when they're still subtle. Someone a little slower to take hints might be faced with an ultimatum of some sort before taking on the challenge. For some reason, *pain* is often the primary motivator when it comes to character growth.

> *Pain is often the primary motivation for character growth.*

The problem is that if people can't readily see the character flaws in their own actions and reactions, then it's difficult or even impossible to success-fully implement some sort of change. Too often, because people aren't really aware that their behavior is caused by a character flaw, they aren't able to solve it on their own. Normally, character development isn't something that comes through self-motivation.

In the context of building a healthy organization, we inevitably have to deal with people whose character flaws are preventing them from being successful, either in their present positions or in positions that they aspire to. There are going to be people who have issues that make others reluctant to work with or for them or make them reluctant to work with others. Once again, we can't engineer our way around re-lationship challenges. We've got to work our way through them ac-cording to the principles and values that we choose to live by.

Healthy organizations realize that they've got to maintain con-sistency all the way up the chain of command in terms of the character of their leaders. There has to be congruence between the organization's value systems and the character qualities of their leaders. Where there are inconsistencies, there are inevitably relationship challenges that affect organizational health. Throughout the entire organization, people have to embrace the value systems that the organization believes are critical to maintaining its culture and its vision. Healthy organizations commit to growth—they own up to and deal with issues that begin to surface as they become aware of them. Beyond self-motivated growth in quality, performance, and customer service areas, there is a real need for leaders who know how to deal appropriately with character issues in the people they lead.

The Left Ditch – On Your Own Dime

At the left extreme of the Learning value, the attitude is one of complete *indifference*. Who cares? If people don't want to grow, what difference does that make? If we don't have to invest anything in them, and they do their job, why would we upset the proverbial apple cart? If people *do* want to grow, let them do it on their own dime—why invest in people who are already capable of doing their jobs adequately?

Well, for one thing, because people are rarely perfect, and they bring their issues and their baggage with them. Most of what consumes our time when we talk about personal growth has little or nothing to do with the skills required to make a better widget or deliver a report on time. The biggest problem is almost always *people*, or more accurately, *relationships between people*. So, if they don't want to grow, or if we think it's none of our business and we shouldn't get involved, that means we're planning on putting up with whatever interpersonal problems we've got now, and we're hoping that they don't affect team camaraderie, morale, quality, customer service, productivity, and profit—which they do.

That's not to suggest that employers are somehow obliged to make sure that the members of every team get along famously with everyone else they have to work with. We're not implying that *responsibility* for how a person thinks, acts, and speaks transfers from the employee to the employer. It's also not to suggest that employers aren't justified in dismissing those who have character flaws that are so significant that it would be better if they learned to resolve them in a different environment. But we *are* suggesting that if organizations want to be healthy, they have to make sure that ignoring character flaws and/or dismissing people with character flaws is not their first line of approach. To avoid dysfunction in this area, they've got to give people a chance to grow.

The Right Ditch – We Know What's Best for You

If the ditch on the left side of the road is to ignore or dismiss people who have character issues, then the ditch on the right is *manipulation*. Manipulative organizations somehow feel that it's incumbent on them to get others to behave in the way that they feel is appropriate, whether others agree or not. Most people hate being manipulated. In fact, manipulation almost always creates a reaction of *defiance*. "You can't make me do it your way, and just to reinforce that, I'm not only going to refuse to do what you want, I'm going to do the opposite!"

To fully understand the challenge, we have to go back to the question of how we value people. Do we view people with character issues as problems? Do we see them as losers who will never amount to anything, or do we pick up the baton and begin to help them see what they can become—help them to find their place in a vision that's larger than they are? Because most of us are not willing to invest in a loser, we have to be careful to look for the potential in people—focus on the future, not the present.

There's a parallel environment that may help to bring some clarity to the issue in the workplace: parents face the same challenges in raising children. Do parents permit character issues to go unchecked because they want to give children the opportunity to "be themselves?" Or, do they make them behave in a certain way, in an attempt to be confident that their children will never embarrass them? Those are the same two ditches on the sides of the same road. Children ignored and left to their own devices may be just as disadvantaged as those raised by dominating parents, more concerned with their own comfort and convenience than with the character of their children. Neglect may be as damaging as manipulation.

Learning-Related Pain Points

There are three practical signs that learning-related dysfunction has begun to set in.

1. Conflict

The most common sign of growth-related dysfunction is unresolved conflict: between departments, leaders, staff, and even the company and its clients or customers. When character flaws are unchecked, or worse yet, when it's taboo to confront them, tensions run high and erupt into open hostility at the slightest provocation.

2. Compensating for inappropriate behavior

Unhealthy organizations waste untold amounts of money and time compensating for their willingness to tolerate inappropriate behavior. We're not talking about a gracious second chance—or even a third or fourth chance. Healthy organizations express commitment and loyalty to employees who make mistakes, while at the same time holding them accountable for the outcomes and consequences of those mistakes. An unhealthy organization doesn't express commitment to employees' growth—it demonstrates its own unwillingness to do anything to help. Unhealthy organizations ignore the problem, hoping that it will disappear, but it rarely does.

3. Employees quit instead of admitting mistakes

Another symptom of growth-related dysfunction is harder to spot, but it has an equally high cost in terms of lost potential, and recruitment and training costs. When employees make mistakes, do they feel that it will be easier for them to quit and find new jobs, or do they feel they will be treated fairly and respectfully if they take responsibility for their errors, or will they be shamed into conformity?

Everyone makes mistakes—there are very few people who would argue that point. And, some of the mistakes that we make are expensive. If an employee fears being humiliated or punished, there's a strong motivation to do all they can to cover up the mistake, attempt to shift the blame to someone else, or even quit before the mistake is caught. The end result? The loss of an opportunity to learn and to grow.

Why does it matter?

Finding a place of balance, where character flaws are dealt with fairly and consistently is critical to organizational health. Organizations that ignore the need for character growth and let the defaults take over have a lot of conflict. A few bossy dictators take over the key roles and then sink the ship. A culture that tolerates people's character flaws attracts people who have them.

Organizations that just eliminate the conflict—make it go away by firing the people who seem to cause it—see a lot of raw talent go out the door—talent they will never get a chance to enjoy. More important, they may have missed the opportunity to do something significant—add tremendous value to a person who might otherwise stumble through life without any real clue as to why they keep hitting the same brick wall. People aren't likely to encourage their friends and family to work for a company where they're going to get fired if they make a mistake!

The Road of Balance

Getting the balance right in our organizations is important for maintaining health. Extremes run a high risk of unhealthy outcomes. Both extremes, indifference and manipulation, tell employees, "Management doesn't care about you." And, the main outcome of both extremes is *conflict*—and lots of it.

In healthy organizations, mistakes are seen as an opportunity to grow. That's not to suggest that you can keep making the same mistake over and over! One of our mentors is fond of saying, "If you're going to make a mistake, at least make a new one!" Handled properly, honest mistakes can be turned from losses into opportunities. Instead of reacting negatively, healthy organizations respond in a supportive way. Healthy organizations also make a point of using mentors to coach staff through the growing process. Mentoring turns mistakes into opportunities; it turns what might have been a waste of time or money into an investment—one that we believe will potentially pay handsome returns.

Encouraging someone to deal with a character weakness is not manipulative.

To find the balance, we believe that leaders need to be willing to invest the mental, emotional, and physical energy needed to become mentors and encouragers. While *telling* someone how they should change and what they *need to become* is manipulative, encouraging someone to deal with a character weakness through reasonable consequences is not.

Case Study

Victor was a project manager who was pretty confident about his abilities and the value he could add to a team. Shortly after starting to work for his employer, he was assigned a pretty difficult project—one that was over budget, behind schedule, and badly off target. Victor had a really cocky, arrogant undertone to his attitude. He saw subordinates and team members as tools that he could use to help him succeed. He saw an opportunity to be a hero and went for it. Victor thought the outcome was a success, but nobody else did! The company lost a lot of business over the fiasco that he created. In the end, his boss had more than "just cause" for dismissal. What our client did next shows amazing foresight.

Instead of firing Victor, the company told him, "Until you learn to serve customers and team members with respect and trust, we will not allow you to have direct communication with any of our customers nor will we allow you to have any supervisory responsibilities. We're here to support you, and we're here to help you. We want you to learn how to do those things, because we think you're going to be an excellent leader—an asset to our team—when you do. But until you do, you're going nowhere." It was pretty clear to Victor that he'd been severely demoted. Victor's boss knew that he had a young family to care for and that cutting his salary would create a lot of hardship for them, so he didn't adjust Victor's salary to match his new position.

Victor says, "I guess I had two choices: I could quit and find a new job or stay and face my mistakes. I had no idea how on earth I was supposed to change, but I could see that they cared enough to give me a chance. In hindsight, it was obvious to me that the damaged relationships I'd left behind were real and that I was responsible for them. Because they were good enough to give me a chance and were essentially willing to pay me to learn, I decided to stay."

Questions

Was the company's choice to support Victor through a time of learning worth it? Wouldn't it have been cheaper for our client to let him go? What sort of message did their choice to work with Victor send to others in the organization? How much trust and loyalty did their decision to work with him create—not just with Victor, but with other staff members too?

We are not responsible to make sure that people grow. That's not something we can guarantee—if we try, we become manipulative. There's an old saying, "You can lead a horse to water, but you can't make him drink." Well, an old farmer added a corollary: "Yeah, but you can salt his oats!" In a healthy organization, leaders see themselves as responsible to ensure that the people they lead develop an appetite for growth and a healthy response to failure—they learn to "salt the oats." Healthy organizations also make sure that people know that the safety net actually works; people can make mistakes, even *big* mistakes, and be treated with respect and dignity.

Confronting with Excellence

Healthy organizations have learned the skill of confronting staff in a way that we call Confronting with Excellence. The key to confronting well is in understanding that it isn't necessary to be angry or upset in order to get results when confronting someone about a mistake or a character issue. Genuinely having the employee's best interest at heart makes it possible to say, "We appreciate you as a person, and we appreciate the contribution you make. We want you to grow and improve, and we want to point out an opportunity for you to increase the value you add to the company, and to your co-workers."

To confront with excellence, it's important to avoid fixing blame. Instead of trying to identify precisely who is at fault for an error, which keeps us focused on the blame side of the equation, the focus needs to be on how each person in the process can grow. Some people respond to confrontation by finding someone else to blame and shifting the focus away from their mistakes. They need to be encouraged to stop the blame game and simply recognize that they can't change how someone else responds to the situation; they can only change their own response. (See Appendix A for an overview you can use to teach the concept of Confronting with Excellence to others.)

The key to success, of course, is that employees have to be convinced that everyone in the organization is getting the same level of feedback, that each person is being challenged to consider their own growth opportunities—they must not feel that they are being singled out or made to be a scapegoat.

How do you manage your own growth? Are you sufficiently self-aware that you can identify one of two specific *character weaknesses* that you know you need to work on personally? Not a plan to learn new skills or gain some sort of accreditation—a plan to address an area of character. Take a few minutes to think about your own character qualities. What are the one or two things that you'd like to work on in the next year?

Summary

The point at which an organization chooses to find the balance point varies. Some organizations choose to lean slightly to the left: when they confront employees over issues of character, they leave a lot of room in terms of *how* people will choose to deal with their issues. Some organizations lean more to the right, involving themselves in the details of an action plan for growth. But in either case, the question is not *if* the organization will choose to mentor staff through the challenges of character growth—the question is *how* and *to what extent* they will give that support.

Employees who work under a balanced system work from a sense of tremendous security. They know that there is tolerance for mistakes and room to grow but recognize the system of accountability at the same time. Under a balanced system, their respect for each other and for leadership goes up dramatically.

Chapter 5:   Unity

Living in Harmony, Celebrating Differences

The sad truth is so many times it is easier to love, forgive, and help others than it is to love, forgive, and accept ourselves.

—Thelma Box

Do you sacrifice your own needs to meet the expectations of others? Do you live by the adage, "Look out for yourself, because no one else will"? Can people live as healthy members of a community while continuing to meet legitimate personal needs?

We label the ditch on the left side of the road for this value Look Out For Number One. By that, we mean that personal benefit weighs in at a significantly higher priority than other considerations. Fundamentally, this ditch is rooted in a sort of selfishness. The people or groups making the decisions make a deliberate choice to deemphasize the concerns or needs of others and focus primarily on themselves. It might not be an aggressive kind of selfishness that deliberately sets out to create a win-lose situation, although that could happen. More often, it's a passive, presumptuous kind of selfishness that simply doesn't take the time to even think about what's good for anyone else.

The ditch on the right side of the road is labeled Yes-Man, reflecting a strong, unhealthy bias toward the out-

People need a nurturing, trusting, fun place where they belong and engage with others.

side community, where the other party's benefit is the only consideration. People who live at this extreme sometimes feel like martyrs who have to give their lives for the sake of the company's cause. They can't keep the appropriate focus on their work because they're constantly getting distracted by opportunities to help others. They're the ones who simply can't bear to say no to an opportunity to help out and then short-change their own needs in the process.

Look Out For Number One (Personal)	Balanced	Yes-Man (Community)
• Little respect for others—it's all about me. • Aggressive in conflict; argumentative environment. • Work to rule.	• Staff feel connected to a clear vision. • Policies are written on a trust model, defining freedoms not restrictions. • Invite feedback from staff in building a healthy work environment.	• Make sacrifices for the good of the company. • Dysfunctional self-denial; don't rock the boat—fit in. • "Martyr Complex"—If I don't do it, nobody will.

Don't assume that the Unity value is what some have called work/life balance. That concept juxtaposes *work* with *life* in a peculiar way, as though when you're working you're not alive; that somehow life pauses when you arrive at the workplace and only resumes again when you leave. The paradox here is not trying to balance the needs of the workplace with the needs and demands of the other communities we belong to. The balance here is between our own needs and expectations and the needs and expectations that we perceive others have. When the balanced range is found, life and work begin to blend into each other in ways that are highly engaging and rewarding. This value has more to do with a self/others balance and a person's ability to juggle the demands of living in a healthy community.

One of our fundamental needs as humans is to live in community. While we're not suggesting that the workplace is the most *important* place where relationships form, in many cases the workplace is the environment where we spend the largest portion of our time. If we can't be fully alive and engaged at work, then neither we nor the organizations we work for can be healthy.

The Left Ditch – Look Out for #1

At the left edge, the deciding factor in every decision is, "What's best for me?" People who live in the left-ditch think primarily about themselves; their concern or regard for what others need is always secondary. Organizations that live at the left extreme focus their purpose exclusively on reaching goals that are good for the company but have little concern for the human cost associated with achieving those goals.

In many ways, the left-ditch is the antithesis of a healthy community. Community doesn't exist when the only purpose that matters to people is their own goals—when they are focused only on establishing and asserting their own identity, and the relationships they attempt to maintain are focused on primarily on meeting their own needs.

A strong distinguishing factor about the left-ditch is the tendency to lean on *rules* to organize life—attempting to structure the complexities of relationship with regulations. Because people in the left-ditch don't want to have to deal with the inevitable messiness of relating to people who have different priorities, likes, and dislikes, they develop a set of rules that define the way they want the interface to work, and then impose those rules on everyone they come into contact with. When those in the left-ditch come up to a relational challenge, they don't seek to understand the other person's perspective; they bring out their rules and seek to enforce the standards that they've developed on the other person.

There are people who choose to live in the left-ditch, but it's much more common to find *organizations* that choose to live there. They focus their mission, vision, and goals on achievements or standards that will set them apart from others, without any real thought for the expectations of the people who make up the organization itself.

Their identity is wrapped up in what they will accomplish, excluding any mention of the sort of community they expect to form or the culture that their organization will embrace and maintain. The very idea that they have a responsibility toward the people who work within the organization doesn't occur to them; there see no relational connection between the organization and its people, between the institution and those who work to assure its success. Their policy manuals govern everything they can regulate, from working hours and sick leave to dress codes and what size desk an employee is allowed to have.

We're not suggesting that an organization doesn't have a *right* to develop specific policies about such things. What we are suggesting, though, is that the policies ought to be written in a way that encourages relational health and allows employees and supervisors to be flexible in the way the policy is applied. Organizations need to be careful that they don't communicate a self-serving attitude; they need to take other's expectations and perceptions into account. Policies ought to presume that people want to do what's right and need some guidance to understand what that is and how it's done. Policies shouldn't presume that people want to do what's wrong, and the company needs regulations to prevent that from happening.

The Right Ditch – Yes-Man

In the right-ditch, people don't think about what *they want* at all. What they want to know is, "How do I make you happy?" People who live at the extreme on the right side of the Unity scale have the idea that it's their responsibility to meet everyone else's needs and that their own needs are irrelevant.

You might think that people who live on the right edge would be only too happy to follow whatever rules those on the left invented to control the relationships around them. Reality is quite different than that. Instead of allowing left-leaning people to regulate every aspect of relationship according to their rules, right-ditch thinking assumes that rules are always restrictive, counter-productive, and unimportant. People who live in the right-ditch refuse to recognize that there is any value to rules or policies at all. What's good for one person may not be good for another; everyone has unique needs and expectations that have to be accommodated somehow. Life is a complicated, messy, and unpredictable place in the right-ditch. (We like to remind people that "no rules" doesn't equal freedom; it equals anarchy. Once again, the key is finding the healthy, balanced range between the two extremes.)

When people live at this extreme, one of the ways they manage to juggle the demands on their own time is to take their own needs and desires completely out of the picture. There's an unhealthy sort of self-abandonment that takes place here. People who live in the right-ditch sacrifice to meet your needs but won't accept the reciprocal gift—they're unwilling to let you give something to them. In contrast, the balanced part of the road is a healthy place of working out a way to reach a win-win position that's good for us and for the people we depend on as well as those who depend on us.

Balance is the place that's good for us and the people who depend on us.

Consider the stay-at-home mom who has spent years sacrificing her own needs for the needs of her children and her husband. One day, something snaps, and she's had enough. When she leaves, what does she say? "I've had it with sacrificing for you guys. When do *I* get some time? When does what *I* want to do count?" Constantly sacrificing our own needs so that we can look after others has its limitations. People who choose to live in the right-ditch in relation to their employer wonder why burnout seems to set in after a while or why their families start to resent the company.

Examples of organizations that live at the right edge of this value system are difficult to find. We think that they do exist, though. The right-ditch may well explain the short life-span of organizations that rally around a social cause but don't last long enough to have any real impact. Their entire purpose is focused on meeting the needs of others. In the short-sighted neglect of their own needs, they run out of money and supporters, or they forget that their own staff members (many of whom may be volunteers) also have needs.

Unity-Related Pain Points

To be healthy, an organization has to help employees find a point of balance between the priority of their personal needs and the needs and expectations of others in the community that is formed by the rest of the organization. We've identified three signs of dysfunction.

1. Resentment

A lot of organizational dysfunction results from right-leaning employees becoming resentful about the policy-driven environment in left-leaning organizations. The organization writes its rules and regulations (policies and procedures) as an attempt to prescribe and regulate the relational interaction between the organization and its staff members. A certain amount of policy is necessary; organizations can't function without it. However, organizations have to be careful about their motives and intentions when writing those policies.

Policy-writers often follow the model they see in our legal system. They write policy that identifies precisely what is and is not acceptable and the consequences that will follow any violation of those expectations. Every time somebody comes up with a loophole or a new twist, a new regulation gets written. The end result communicates to staff members that they aren't trusted to do what's right and that the company doesn't believe they will treat its interests with integrity. We're not suggesting that the organization sets out to communicate such a lack of trust, but it's the message people end up hearing.

The outcome is resentment. People who are told (even inadvertently) that they aren't trustworthy tend to become resentful of every new policy that they see as reinforcing that message. Instead of seeing policies as guidelines that help them to be consistent in the way they handle things, they see them as an insult—an attempt to regulate or legislate the integrity they would otherwise have offered freely. (The policy-writers also become resentful over all the clever ways people find to get around the rules they're trying to build!)

2. Low respect for others

Turf wars and silos are the result of employees who forget that they're "on the same team." If the star player on a team breaks his personal scoring record for a single game, but his team loses to their opponents, he may have had his best game ever, but he still lost. When one part of the organization wins at the expense of another, the same thing happens. Those are signs that parts of the organization have forgotten that they belong to a larger community and have begun to prioritize their own success at the expense of the community's success.

When there's a strong sense of community, there's a natural willingness to share resources, ideas, and solutions. Win-lose situations where one part of the organization wins at the expense of another are rare when there's a strong sense of belonging to a bigger vision. As a result, respect and service flourish in healthy organizations. Low respect for others, whether directed toward supervisors, co-workers, or subordinates indicates that people don't understand their relationship to the community and how their involvement benefits the company as a whole.

3. Low commitment

Regardless of how committed new employees are to the company—willing to make sacrifices and do what it takes to get the job done—it doesn't last long in an unhealthy organization. It doesn't take long for new staff members to realize that there are people around them who've been there a while who aren't giving as much as they do. And it doesn't take them long to find out why.

An organization that doesn't promote healthy balance might think that it's getting "free" extra effort from employees, but the "bonus" is usually short-lived. If employees aren't encouraged to balance extra effort during busy times with extra time off during slower times, for example, they begin to feel used and undervalued. People who feel like they aren't important are unwilling to make sacrifices. Employees aren't about to give up their own time and agendas for a company that never seems to be willing to reciprocate.

Why does it matter?

Again, what are the real and practical effects of building a healthy community in the workplace? Remember, the point is not to find a right or wrong answer. While it's relatively obvious that being out of balance is unhealthy, the question of exactly where to establish the balance point remains up to each organization to decide. It's well known that people do better when they live in community than when they live in isolation. The synergy that results from working in healthy relationships with others brings huge benefits with it. For that reason, and because most organizations tend to lean too far to the left, we encourage our clients to lean toward the right side of the road on this value. We encourage them to work harder than they think they need to at making sure that the balance is there and that the personal needs of employees get proper time and focus.

Organizations need to work hard at defining the kind of community they want, and then craft their policies and procedures around that cultural standard. The culture needs to be designed and implemented with every bit as much care and attention as the business practices themselves. When the culture sets the expectations and guidelines that help employees decide how they will balance the Unity value, stress levels go down and trust, commitment, and performance go up.

The Road of Balance

How do we find the place of balance? Somehow, somewhere in our thinking, there's a process that we use to determine what we're going to sacrifice and what we're going to keep. When there's a dilemma, we make value judgments that decide what's more important. We're going to pay a price either way, so we figure out which option we feel is better and accept the outcome. The question is not so much *what* we decide because that probably changes from situation to situation. The more important issue is *how* we decide or why we make the decision that we do.

To be healthy, organizations need to help their staff members understand the intentions behind policies and guidelines. They need to communicate the why with as much clarity as they communicate the what. In developing policies, organizations need to work from a foundation of trust. It's best to write policies as guidelines that give properly motivated employees a rule of thumb that they can use as a way of understanding what the organization's leaders would like them to do in a given situation. That way, supervisors and managers can use their own wisdom and discretion in applying the policies in a way that honors the original intent, applying that intention to the specifics of the present situation. When someone attempts to abuse the policy, twisting it so that it gives them something that's outside of what was intended, the organization needs to deal with that as an exception.

There's a subtle macro-level implication to the way an organization chooses to live out this value system. Companies face the same need to choose between what's best for them and for the communities that they live in. Being a "good corporate citizen" means that companies have to remember to balance the needs of the communities they live and operate in with their own needs. There are plenty of examples of companies who have chosen to prioritize profits over taking care of the environment and people around them. At the other end of the scale, we've already mentioned the organizations that have pushed hard for the communities around them but forgot to look after themselves.

Organizations can bring balance to this area in a number of ways:

> When employees know the company genuinely cares about them and wants them to live balanced lives, they're more willing to support each other in bringing that balance to the workplace. One organization we know tells employees, "When it's slow, we expect you to rest hard! Because when it's busy, we expect you to work hard!" They actually encourage employees to go home early or come in late and take extended lunch breaks when things are a little slow. It's amazing to see how readily those same employees come early, stay late, and eat lunch at their desks when it's busy.

> Companies need to be willing to bring in contract or temporary help when the workload increases. When considering the cost of bringing in extra help, remember that using employees to get that same work done isn't free—beyond the cost of overtime, there are the intangible costs of pulling employees off of their point of balance for more than a short period of time. While those costs are hard to measure, they are very real.

> It may be possible to encourage employees in other departments to "roll up their sleeves" and help out with extra workloads. If the salespeople have done well but now the shipping department is swamped, there's an opportunity to building camaraderie between the two—the salespeople might discover that it's harder than they thought in the shipping department, and the staff in the warehouse might really appreciate the fact that the salespeople are willing to help solve a problem that, in their perception, sales staff created in the first place! Instead of reinforcing an "us and them" mentality (which is indicative of

an out-of-balance position), the opportunity can actually *build* community.

Case Study

Sabrina worked for a local bank for fifteen years, surviving one merger after another. She was now working part-time in order to invest her time in other priorities in her life.

In the early years of her career, Sabrina knew her team leaders, and they knew her. They had clear practices and procedures for serving clients and protecting shareholder assets. Those policies were clear, precise, and highly structured. However, what Sabrina refers to as "People Practices" were very open, simple, and trusting.

There were three basic guidelines: take time to develop yourself, be reasonable and appropriate in dealing with fellow staff, and keep commitments. The team always seemed to make it work. When she needed to have some time off, her boss would smile and say, "Have your commitments been met?" For Sabrina, life at the bank was great—the kind of place she recommended to her friends.

After the last merger things really changed: much more formal human resources policies came down to the branch from the new head office. The team leader resisted the culture change and was replaced. The new team leader was an eager ambassador of the new rule book. Sabrina asked if the three principles—develop yourself, be reasonable, and keep commitments—made sense. The new team leader just shrugged her shoulders and said something about too much freedom creating unwieldy teams. Defined systems and processes were better, in her opinion.

The rules were met with all the creative resistance the staff was capable of. Weekly interpretation bulletins were sent to the branches to ensure consistent compliance. Sabrina, still working at the same branch, now easily spends an hour each week reading and signing off interpretation bulletins. She only works twenty-four hours in a week and says, "I can't believe it takes an hour just to read the latest and greatest plug for the loophole some staff member found."

"Work is no longer fun," says Sabrina. She wonders why all the policies, case laws, and interpretation bulletins matter. She's suspicious and unmotivated. She's never been one to gossip but finds herself sharing her disappointment openly with others who readily agree. Sabrina wants out—she's looking for a healthy organization.

Questions

What's at the heart of Sabrina's growing disillusion with her workplace? Why do you think the three basic guidelines worked so well? Why do you think people write such long, arduous and controlling rules?

Have you ever taken the time to consider what the heart of a policy or procedure should really be? Consider the policies and procedures in your own organization: do you use policies to control staff, or are they designed to give them freedom to work within clear boundaries?

Conflict Resolution

One of the things that every community has to deal with at some level is resolving conflict between members of the community. People who see things differently inevitably run into differences of opinion about what's important, how something should be done, or how to handle inequity. The left-leaning people will usually point to the need for something written that arbitrates those disagreements in a consistent way. Right-leaning people are more likely to feel that, given time, everything will "come out in the wash." What they often hope is that things will equalize themselves over a range of different circumstances.

How should these things be handled? What should organizations do to provide staff members with a framework for handling conflict? There is a case to be made for writing policies that address commonly occurring problems; there's no point having supervisors or managers involved in adjudicating every situation where a few employees have to decide whose turn it is to do the job nobody really wants, for example. However, we strongly recommend that our clients resist the urge to write policies that are specific and focus their attention on the *process* for resolving conflict instead of attempting to write policies that predetermine the *outcomes*. Here's the basic framework:

➤ Specify terminology that helps staff members differentiate between concerns and issues. When staff members have a *concern*, all they're looking for is to be heard. They simply want the assurance that someone with some authority has listened to what they said and is willing to consider their input. When staff members have an *issue*, they're saying that they actually expect a supervisor or manager to take some specific action on the item they've brought forward. They want something more than just a sympathetic ear.

➤ When a staff member tables an issue, supervisors are *required* to address it. If resolving the issue is beyond their authority, they must escalate it and hold others in the organization accountable for addressing it. How the issue gets addressed isn't specified by the policy; the policy only states that once it's raised, it gets duly logged, escalated to management if necessary, and must be addressed in writing. (It works best when senior managers keep track of the number of outstanding issues and keep asking for updates on any issue that's more than a few weeks old.)

➤ Once an issue has been addressed, the decision or outcome is communicated back to the originating staff member's supervisor, who goes over the response with the employee. If the employee isn't happy, and he or she can show the supervisor that the decision didn't take some fairly important piece of information into account, there's one chance for an appeal. Beyond that, the outcome of the process is final.

Once again, organizations need to resist the urge to take the decisions that come out of the issues resolution process and turn them into policies. It's the *process* that gives staff members the confidence that when they have an issue, they can get it addressed in an objective way. Our clients are often surprised at how much more efficient it is to address issues one by one than it is to spend the effort developing policies to try and address the same problems. The intangible benefits are huge: by taking a position farther to the right on the Unity scale, moving from exclusive use of rules toward more acceptance of relational concerns, employees feel that the company has a much more caring approach toward them and is going to listen when they feel they have something to say.

Summary

In many ways, the Unity value is about the culture of the organization—the community that forms inside the company. Employees who work under a balanced system are convinced that the company actually *cares* about them as a person, and in return, they actually *care* about what happens to the company. By extension, they care more about each other too. Companies who insist on staying near the left edge, who work hard at making sure that their staff members will do exactly what's expected of them, often end up with a toxic culture that puts them at odds with the very people they hope will make them successful. Instead of building alliances with their staff members, they try to control them; instead of treating them as valuable partners, they see them as pawns.

The word *organization* shares a common root with the words organic and organism. Corporate leaders need to remember that. Remember that 100 percent of the staff members in our companies are *people*. Understanding how relationships work and making sure that we structure our policies according to relational principles and values is critical to building a healthy culture.

Chapter 6:   Empathy

Responding to the needs of others

On a winter night in a rural area, an Amish family was doing their evening chores. Two boys were hard at work in the loft of the barn, forking hay down to the animals below, when one of them accidentally knocked the coal oil lantern from its hook. The fire spread so quickly in the dry hay that the father, who was working nearby, only had time to rescue his sons from its intensity. Everything else was lost.

A few months later, in early summer, more than 400 Amish men from various communities converged on the farm, not only to rebuild the barn (in a single day) but also to stock it with hay for the coming year.

Everyone goes through times where they need a little help. Sometimes life dishes out such a storm that a lot of help is necessary. Sometimes help means just having somebody there to offer support. Other times, it means we need to add financial support or professional help to the friendship and moral support we can offer on our own. EAP (Employee Assistance Programs) or EFAP (which adds the word *family* to the mix) only go so far and sometimes have the reputation of being simply a necessity that doesn't really meet the need, like putting a bandage on a bullet hole.[5]

Do you feel that people who receive charity should be held accountable for how they use it? Do you believe that people who experience difficulty are often victims of circumstance, and will make responsible choices if they get another chance?

People need support to help them get through challenging times.

For Empathy, the ditch on the left side of the road is labeled Hard-Liner. At this extreme, when someone needs help or support, the focus is on accountability (in the strongest possible connotation.)To get help, you need to have a plan that shows a clear return on investment. The company expects that whatever support you get will be paid back somehow—not necessarily in cash but certainly in increased effort and loyalty in the future. The organization is willing to support you but only if there's some way to show that there's an "upside" to their investment.

The ditch on the right side of the road is labeled Bleeding Heart. It describes charity in the extreme sense—simple donations without any expectation or follow-up. When someone comes into an unfortunate situation and needs help, immediate relief is offered, but there's no real commitment to helping in the longer term.

Hard-Liner (Accountability)	Balanced	Bleeding Heart (Charity)
• No one gets help without a clear plan. • Emphasis is on eliminating problems without addressing symptoms. • Needs are seen as due to negligence.	• Support is more than financial—it includes coaching and mentoring. • Provide access to professional support staff. • Immediate relief is coupled to long-term problem solving.	• Co-facilitators of dysfunctional behavior; want to help, but perpetuate the problem. • Address symptoms without considering the cure. • Highly susceptible to fraudulent claims.

The challenges of life can have a profound affect on employee productivity, job safety, and work quality. For example, conflict with a spouse or a teenage son or daughter on the way to work can poison a whole day. Having a family member who's experiencing a health challenge is a nagging problem that most people can't simply put out of their minds while they do their jobs. But what kind of help are we supposed to offer? What can we realistically do? What if an employee's problems seem self-created—drugs or alcohol abuse, for instance? Are we still obliged to get involved? Could our generosity have the unfortunate effect of making the problem worse? How much help is enough, and what are the limits?

These are all tough questions, especially when we put them into the context of the workplace. Once again, there's a paradox here—two extremes that we need to avoid as we find a place of balance where we get out of the ditches and onto the road.

The Empathy value generates more strong opinions than any other system. It seems to us that many people align their thinking with the far left and right ends of the scale, and few are willing to do the work of understanding each other deeply enough to find the range of balance in the middle. Yet, it is the place of balance where organizations can find the way to create a healthy and supportive response to their staff members when needs arise.

The Left Ditch – Hard-Liner

People whose thinking puts them at left end of the Empathy value scale feel that it's important to understand *why* help is needed and *how* they are expected to help before they are willing to offer assistance. It's not that they are unwilling to help—in fact, they can be very generous when their concerns about causes and prevention are addressed. But they place their emphasis on making sure that whatever assistance they offer won't be abused, contribute to further problems, or be like "pouring money and effort into a bottomless pit."

As with the other value scales, there are positions and ways of thinking that are so far to the left, they are "in the ditch." There are a few people—more commonly, there are a few organizations—that are nothing short of callous or hard-hearted about their willingness to offer assistance to people with needs. Before they help, they want a sense that the recipients are willing to accept responsibility for their mistakes and give some sort of account or explanation as to how the help they hope to receive will work toward eliminating a reoccurrence of the need.

That sort of thinking can infuriate people who think along the right side of the scale; in fact, it can seem absolutely unconscionable. The idea that someone who is the victim of an unfortunate circumstance should be forced to accept some sort of responsibility for their problem seems ludicrous. "Are you trying to tell me that if someone in your family is dying of cancer, that's somehow supposed to be *somebody's fault?*" they ask incredulously.

And, they're right of course. Very few people whose thinking leans left would disagree with them. Most of the people who lean to the left don't lean so far left that they fall into the ditch. Much more commonly, left-leaning people will do what they can to help, but they have nagging concerns that somehow, somebody needs to think about what sort of precedents are being set, and how much long-term money and effort is being committed in deciding to offer support to people with what are clearly valid needs. They want to know how to make sure that there's enough money for future needs and how to make sure that there's some sort of equity in the distribution system. They worry about whether or not there's an unhealthy dependency being created. They're concerned about abuse and the possibility that someone who isn't actually entitled to assistance will take money out of the system, leaving less for the valid needs.

Of course there are times when the left-leaning position has more to do with insensitivity than it does with frugality. The people who control the spending in an organization may be so far away from the ones who need support that they are simply unaware of the opportunity to help in a meaningful way. They might have good intentions and a willingness to help, but they have no way of knowing where and when help is needed and no way of gauging how help in an appropriate way.

As an aside, organizations embrace insurance-based EAP or EFAP programs, because they move both the costs and the detection to a third party provider. By doing so, they push the question of detecting need into the hands of the people who need the help; they can dial a toll-free number and talk to someone who will hopefully provide the appropriate response. The programs also take much of the uncertainty out of the cost of providing help. Insurance programs come with a predictable premium that lends itself nicely to the budgeting process. Don't presume that left-leaning companies are the only ones that find those programs attractive; right-leaning companies like them too, but for different reasons.

The Right Ditch – Bleeding Heart

At the right end of the scale are those who feel that people with unfortunate problems in life are largely victims of circumstance and asking them to put some form of explanation or accountability on the help they receive is further victimizing them. The extreme right end of the scale reads like a communist manifesto: transfer all the wealth of the rich to the poor through generous social programs and support systems. Left-leaning people cringe at the very idea. They're thankful that such extreme philosophies are rare in North America.

Much more common, though, is the right-ditch perspective where people find themselves moved toward action for the homeless or jobless person standing on the street corner with a cardboard sign, hoping for enough donations to provide the next meal. Instead of *thinking*, "Somebody should do something here," they find satisfaction in knowing that they actually *did* something that made a difference. The dollar or two they put into the person's hand is part of the solution—a small part perhaps, but at least they've done something. Left-ditch thinking scoffs at the idea that giving a dollar or two makes a difference. They are likely to be the ones who mutter, "Get a job, you bum!" as they go by. To those on the extreme left, the person holding the sign isn't "unemployed," he's *lazy*. Giving him a dollar or two isn't "helping," it's facilitating a poor choice. Right-ditch perspectives don't worry about whether or not their generosity is facilitating poor choices—they respond to the request for help. They are discharging *their obligation* to help, without worrying about any obligation the recipient may have in the process or unhealthy dependencies they may be creating.

As we hinted earlier, right-leaning organizations move to insurance programs as quickly as left-leaning ones do. To them, having a generous insurance program that makes funds and professional services available to their staff members is a way of ensuring that their desire to be supportive and helpful is well served. The toll-free number is a way they can make sure that there is unrestricted access to the system, and they're happy to contribute their share of the premiums. Often, right-leaning organizations don't limit their involvement to the insurance program. To them, insurance is only part of the answer.

The Left-Right Controversy

The controversy between the two viewpoints is practical and real. It plays out almost every day in editorials, blogs, and the opinions of broadcasters. It's a regular topic at the water cooler and social gatherings almost everywhere across the country. It's a constant concern for politicians, governments, and regulators. Whether the topic is affordable housing for the "working poor," budgets for health care, or "means tests" as part of qualifying for financial assistance, the opinions at both extremes are plentiful. And once again, neither of the extremes is particularly helpful.

The idea that accountability—feedback and explanation designed to ensure that gifts are used wisely—is the ultimate cure assumes that someone is to blame for every situation, which we know is false. Those who tend to think that way toward others might change their philosophy in a heartbeat if they found themselves the ones needing support one day.

At the same time, the idea that money solves every problem is equally short-sighted. What about the employee who is going through a marital breakdown or some other relational crisis? How does money or time off solve that? It can pay for a counselor, but does that tell the employee that someone actually *cares*? Some time off might be welcome, but does it actually relieve the problem?

In the real world, problems have a way of sneaking up on us. Seemingly, out of nowhere, we suddenly need help. Even chronic problems, things that have been going on for a while, can suddenly spin out of control.

When most of our society lived in agricultural communities, there may have been more understanding for people who had needs. In an agricultural setting, results take time. Farmers plant seed, and then they wait. They water the seed, and then they wait. They pick weeds, and then they wait. They weather a few storms, and they wait some more. Finally, the crop is ripe, and they collect the harvest—the results. We hate to wait! We like a mechanical paradigm better than an agricultural one. Simply find what's wrong and fix it. No waiting; no patience required. If the mechanic tells us we have to wait until tomorrow before he can get the part, we grumble at how long it took.

Unfortunately, helping people solve problems, especially personal problems, looks more like agriculture than mechanics. It doesn't work to sit someone down, figure out what's broken, pop in a new part (a new way of thinking, environment, or set of reactions), and send them off working properly again. To actually help, there has to be an investment of *time* and *relational effort* in the process. Perhaps as an unfortunate side effect of our present-day concerns about privacy and confidentiality, the help we give today is based little on personal support and primarily on financial assistance. Anonymity for both donor and recipient has eliminated the personal advice and support that may have accompanied a gift in times past.

As with the other value systems, there isn't a specific spot on the scale that's guaranteed to be healthy. If our organizations are going to be healthy, we have to live with *some* form of balance. The extremes create disagreement and dysfunction. Only when we reach as widely as possible do we find a basis for agreement.

Empathy-Related Pain Points

Probably the most significant indicator of empathy-related dysfunction in an organization is the level of cynicism among employees about the company's likelihood to offer meaningful support when it's needed. It's a soft measurement, but it's a clear warning sign. When staff feels like the company is going to "be there for them" if and when times get tough, that message has a way of spreading warmly through the stories that are told at the coffee machine, water cooler, or lunch room. When the company has the opposite reputation, cynicism replaces warmth. Look at these three areas to evaluate empathy.

1. Unsupportive policies or cultures

A quick look at the policies related to employee assistance, family assistance, and time off for compassionate leave or maternity/paternity leave will tell you where the organization stands in terms of their internal value system. How much leeway do supervisors have in terms of applying the policies? Do they have the authority to grant extra time off, if, in their opinion, an employee needs it? Can they give time off when the situation doesn't *exactly* fit the definition in the policy? Do they have the ability to draw on other resources to fill in for a missing worker on short notice? Can employees maintain a certain level of anonymity when they need to draw on programs, if they feel that there is potential embarrassment involved?

The real question here is this: Have the leaders in the organization *predetermined* that they will stand with staff members when trouble hits?

➢ Have leaders decided ahead of time that they will be supportive, available, and willing to provide the best resources and advice they can, when staff members have needs?

➢ Are policies written from the perspective of guiding supervisors to make decisions that prioritize support for staff members?

➢ Are they flexible enough that they do not presuppose blame?

In unhealthy organizations, the focus is on protecting the organization's interests in the event that an employee unexpectedly becomes unable to work or unavailable for work, making sure that the company's risk is minimized. In healthy organizations, such policies are written from the perspective of making sure that employee's immediate needs are cared for, giving supervisors guidelines for ensuring that consequential disruptions and costs are minimized *without* compromising the support offered to staff. If employees are going to be unavailable for longer than the time expected under the policy, there are clear guidelines that explain how the necessary support can be extended.

2. Blame orientation

In unhealthy organizations and cultures, there's a value system that demands someone "take the blame" for every situation where money needs to be spent to "fix a mistake." Somehow, identifying who is at fault is more important than solving the problem, and pinning the blame is more important than figuring out the appropriate response.

Don't assume that somehow, by implication, healthy organizations are soft on mistakes. In organizations where there's balance on the scale of empathy, the standards are actually higher, and the accountability for mistakes is actually stronger! Why? Because when people know that the company is gracious about holding them accountable for mistakes, and know that the focus is going to be on improving the processes not on finding someone to blame, they're more likely to embrace the process and become objective themselves.

3. Enabling poor behavior

A simple example helps to clarify this third pain point: some parents would rather give their teens money to go and have pizza with their friends than spend time with them. Their logic is that it's been a tough day and they're tired, so they're not up to the noise and the inevitable arguments. When that becomes a regular habit, the pattern has a strongly negative effect on the well-being of the teens.

There are organizations that effectively do the same thing. Instead of making sure they have healthy, open, honest communication with their employees, they try to ignore the problems and throw money at them when they get annoying or embarrassing. Instead of *helping*, what they do is create a culture of *lawlessness*, a culture that attracts people who abuse the system, corrupts people who are easily swayed, and repels people who have integrity—hard workers are offended by "slackers" or others whose performance is suboptimal.

Why does it matter?

So why address the whole issue of empathy at all? Social assistance programs abound in our society, health care is relatively easy to access, and professional counselors are readily available. Isn't it enough to give people time and space to deal with their personal crisis—maybe hold a position open for them for a while? Is there some sort of responsibility to become personally involved in helping them through their crisis?

The answer is simple: one of the most practical ways to demonstrate to a person that you value their inherent worth rather than simply appreciating their economic value is to invest in them without a motive of return on that investment.

The Road of Balance

So, what is the range of balance? How do we provide the support people need without enabling inappropriate or unacceptable behavior among the few who try to take advantage of the system? How do we deliver support effectively, without making it awkward or embarrassing for those who have already been hit with unfortunate or tragic situations?

First, it takes *courage* to be willing to step into a situation and offer help. It's much easier to walk away thinking, "I have enough problems of my own without helping someone else." Helping someone solve a problem, especially a big problem, is not for the faint of heart. Second, it takes *wisdom* to know when you're able to help and when the problem is so big it needs to be given to a professional or someone trained to deal with it. Third, it takes *commitment* to be effective. It's not a good idea to step into someone's situation, help them for a while, and then decide that this is really taking too much time. All of that presumes you *care* enough to actually notice someone needs help in the first place!

Once we focus upon these three requirements for balance it becomes apparent that both the left and right-ditch responses to the empathy value issues are overly mechanical. They simply do not take the time for the human interaction necessary in order to give a balanced empathetic response to situations.

The road of balance also realizes treating symptoms is never as effective as solving problems. It's easier, and it seems like it will be quicker, but it never lasts. It takes time to understand the real problem and work at finding a solution. That doesn't mean treating symptoms isn't important! The dentist's anesthetic doesn't fix the decayed tooth. Removing the decay and filling the tooth is the more permanent cure. However, without the anesthetic, getting the tooth filled may simply be unbearable!

The analogy is useful. Sometimes the best sort of help is to provide welcome relief immediately. Whether that means money for some professional counsel or time off to recover, it provides the buffer or the space that employees need to begin the process of getting through a difficult time. But, it can't end there. When employees access the help system for something, they need to feel that the process is a genuine expression of concern for their well-being as a member of the community. Most people are surprisingly good at reading motives, and intuitively know when someone is trying to "brush them off," or when an expression of concern isn't genuine. In light of that, the company needs to ensure that the system of accountability for the help is not based on a return on their investment. In other words, *don't invest in people hoping for a return; do it because it's the right thing to do.* If employees are somehow obliged to "make it worth the company's effort" when help is given, there's going to be a lot of resentment attached to the program.

That doesn't mean the help can't come with strings attached, though. It's not unreasonable, for example, to insist that if problems persist and more money or time off seems necessary, the employees need to meet with a professional who will then advise the company on what sort of help will be most effective.

Empathy *Inside* the Workplace

Empathy goes far beyond situations where employees need time or assistance to deal with issues that happen *outside* of the workplace. It's a pervasive value. Organizations that are generous tend to be understanding and gracious in situations that are work-related as well.

There's a corporate myth[6] about someone who made a "multi-million dollar mistake." Instead of firing the employee responsible for the error, management's response was, "Why would we fire you after we've just invested millions in a training program of which you are the primary beneficiary?" Obviously, firing the responsible employee would have done nothing to recover the loss. In fact, it might have the opposite effect if he left to work for a competitor! Seeing a loss as an investment in a training program is a way of turning a disaster into a stepping stone. That happens in companies where generosity is part of the corporate value system and employees are basically believed to be competent—both signs of a balanced perspective on the Empathy value scale.

Case Study

Jonathan lost his father to cancer and took it very hard. He was not doing well getting through the grieving process. His compassionate leave had already been extended to give him a little more time to get through his emotions, but it was pretty obvious that he simply was not ready to return to work. He'd already used up the time that the HR policy on time off permitted and was hoping that his supervisor would give him a few more days. Jonathan's supervisor told him, "Take as much time off with pay as you need. Don't worry about the time off policy. But, you need to do something for me. Because we're committed to helping you get through this, we want you to see someone for some grief counseling. We want you to get professional help." Then, the company kept paying the counseling bills for several weeks—well past the time when he successfully returned to work.

If they were right-ditch, the company could have given the employee another week off, hoping that would help. If they were left-ditch, they might have been a bit put out with Jonathan's inability to return to work. Jonathan's employer was able to provide support, without judging and without discriminating. At the same time, an accountability mechanism was created to make sure that the help was *actually helping*. So often the notion of accountability evokes images of charity police checking up to make sure that no one is wasting the money they were given. That's clearly not what's needed. In healthy organizations, there's a process for making sure that the money being spent and the time being invested is actually moving toward a solution, and not just prolonging the pain.

Questions

What is your tendency in dealing with staff who encounter hardships? What message does your reaction send to your staff? What is your initial reaction to the financial and time position that the company took in Jonathan's situation? Why did you feel this way?

Think of a time when you wished you'd had the kind of support from your employer that Jonathan did, but didn't receive it—did you stay with the company? Did it change your attitude toward them?

Practical approaches

Let's not forget the proverb, "An ounce of prevention is worth a pound of cure." Instead of waiting until employees have to deal with the strain and stress of a difficult home, why not offer courses designed to help people cope with the normal stresses of family life? That's just one example, and there are lots of others:

➢ Offer courses or coaching for families with young children to help parents deal with stress.

➢ Work with alcohol and drug abuse counselors and do preventive work instead of waiting for problems to arise. Encourage parents of pre-teen children to take the workshops as a way of helping them to recognize danger signs.

➢ Offer incentives for employees who improve their overall fitness—such as time off with pay to run in a marathon, for example—and offer no-charge access to nutritionists for those who have weight problems.

➢ Let employees invite family members for presentations or programs; don't make them for staff members only.

If you know that an employee is facing a particular issue, you might even make attendance in one of these programs mandatory during regular office hours.

Summary

Employees who work under a balanced system work from a sense of being genuinely valued. Balance in this value system is one of the most practical ways to demonstrate people's inherent worth—it's not just their ability to contribute on the job. Families of employees who work under a well balanced system genuinely appreciate the employer and are much less likely to complain when sacrifices are made for the employer, because they know that the employer is willing to reciprocate.

Section 2:
Building Healthy Organizations

The first section asks questions about organizational dysfunction and describes what it looks and feels like. The five value systems establish a baseline for understanding the components of organizational health. This section addresses where and how to find balance on each of the values. It's important to restate our opinion that the balance isn't found in at specific point.

No matter which spot you pick along any of the five value scales, that spot will reflect a *bias*. Having a bias isn't necessarily a bad thing, as long as you're aware that you have one. Bias isn't necessarily a problem for an organization either, provided that they understand that their bias means they have a spot that they prefer strongly enough that they more or less insist that everyone on the staff embraces the same choices as they do.

What we prefer to move toward is a balanced range; a more broadly minded perspective that allows for the fact that different people see the balance between the left and right ends of the scales in different ways. In healthy organizations, there's a deliberate willingness—sometimes even a deliberate *strategy*—to encourage people to reach out and partner with someone who has an opposing point of view. Choosing to partner with someone who sees things differently allows us to put ourselves in their shoes for a while and see things through their eyes. Does that create conflict? Only if we aren't willing to place value on someone who disagrees with us, or if we aren't secure enough in our own self-worth and feel that our opinion must be the *right one* all the time.

Let's think about a healthy organization and describe what we find. The leaders in healthy organizations do five things. The healthier they are, the better they do them.

1. *They value people—all people.*

They value customers, staff, suppliers, and even their competitors. They insist that everyone demonstrates a commitment to value others, not just someone who has some kind of title. They refuse to put up with people who devalue others. If someone's way to look more important is to make someone else look less important, there is a predictable confrontation about that attitude.

2. *Leaders focus on making sure every member is working where they fit.*

Leaders in these organizations also realize that one of the ways to show value for people is to help them be successful. They not only insist on showing value, they strongly encourage people to live up to their potential. People's gifts match their responsibilities, and their output matches their capability. When someone isn't functioning at the level they know is possible, they do their best to find out why and provide whatever support is needed to get them back on top of their game. Leaders at every level are quick to sit down with someone and talk about what they expect when a person isn't living up to expectations. But they don't do it with a selfish motive; they do it because they genuinely care that each person is fully engaged and motivated to do their best.

3. *Leaders strongly encourage growth.*

Skills, character, profit, product improvement—everything needs to grow. And most of the time, growing means people need to find out what they do best and focus on improving it. Find the strengths and grow even stronger. Integrity underscores everything they do—the broad definition of integrity that not only includes honesty and trustworthiness, but also the ability to embrace difficulty and grow and be authentic about strengths and weaknesses.[7]

4. They deliberately create a healthy, energizing, and positive culture in the workplace.

They realize that if people are going to be productive, they have to belong to a community that's supportive and encouraging. They make sure that policies are guidelines, not rules, and that they are applied in ways that are respectful and supportive. They make sure that there are healthy ways to address conflict and issues in the workplace. They work hard at building a rich, relational environment.

5. The leaders care.

They give selflessly and generously in ways that make a difference. They've decided that they are "all in" before they even become aware of a need. When someone hurts, there's no question about whether or not they're going to help, and the commitment is infectious. Their example encourages everyone to contribute. Some put in extra effort on the job, some contribute by donating money, some contribute by bringing over a supper or mowing a lawn or helping in another practical way, but everyone recognizes that they have an obligation to help where they can. There is no tolerance for stinginess—once again, that attitude will be confronted. Why? Because they know that the person who is stingy in giving will also be reluctant to ask for help. When the tables turn and they're the ones who need support, they'll try to be heroes and get through it on their own. People who see life that way are loners, and loners don't make good team players.

Applying V.A.L.U.E. to Others

Leaders in healthy organizations deliberately design a culture that embeds these values and insist that people live them out. If people can't or won't live them out, then they won't last in the organization—they'll feel uncomfortable or out of step. It's that simple. The culture they design goes well beyond the front door of the office, the walls of the warehouse, or the fence around the yard. It applies to virtually everyone and everything that they come into contact with. Each of those five values becomes pervasive in their culture. The values percolate through the entire fabric of the organization, and become part of the motive behind almost every decision.

Customers are valuable because they're people, not just because they buy stuff. They're people with real problems that need real solutions. And because the organization is expected to deliver the solution, they deliver the best quality they can, for the best price they can, the best way they can, because the customer is worth it. They don't devalue a customer by overpromising, under-delivering or overcharging. Why? Because customers are people, and people are valuable, and they don't treat something valuable carelessly.

The values are pervasive—they influence the entire culture.

They help customers grow. They don't only try to meet the customer's present needs, they help them look ahead and figure out what they will need to grow and what they will need after they've grown. Then, they feed that back into their own growth cycle so that they'll be able to provide the products and the services that the customer will need for a long time. Making sure that the organization is growing is seen as part of what allows them to continue to serve customers well.

They make sure that customers feel like they are part of the community—they have events where customers can meet each other and where staff can interact with customers outside of a work environment. They reinforce the fact that there can't be an "us and them" relationship between staff and customers. When a customer has a problem, they have a problem. When the customer has a win, they help celebrate. Policies aren't seen as rules that customers are expected to abide by; they're guidelines that help staff ensure that customers are well served and treated with respect. There's a strong sense of synergy between the organization and its customers, and it flows out of the synergy that exists within the organization itself.

It doesn't stop there. The people in healthy organizations treat everyone they deal with that way. Why? Because it's the right way to treat people! And if it's right in one environment, then it's right all the time. In fact, they treat *themselves* that way—they are convinced that what they supply or produce has value. They're not willing to charge less than they should or produce more than they reasonably can, because they know that the company needs to survive and prosper if it's going to continue to serve customers well. Let's face it: going out of business is *not* serving customers well, in fact, breaking even does not serve customers well either because there is no money for development.

Chapter 7: Finding the Balance

How do we actually find the place where the balanced range works? How do we get people to start thinking about opinions that are different than their own in a way that adds *strength* instead of *conflict*? The purpose of this chapter is to describe a healthy organization and the way that the values actually come to life there. We hope that by the time you finish reading this chapter, you'll be ready to start measuring the health of your organization and building plans and strategies for making it as healthy as you possibly can.

Value: What Are People Worth?

Where's the balance between valuing people for who they are and valuing them for what they produce? People want to be valued. When they know they are appreciated for who they are, they tend to respond by living up to expectations of them in terms of performance. When they know the organization is adding value to them, they tend to reciprocate and add value to the organization. Where people are valued, trust increases. Where trust increases, decisions are quicker and easier to make. Decisions are better, too, because collaboration is much more natural when trust is high. People who feel undervalued or sense that an employer is using them reciprocate by holding back what they might otherwise have contributed.

If organizations are afraid of putting a lot of energy and effort into making sure that people are genuinely valued, they're not going to be able to get productivity to the place they know it should be, and they're guilty of believing a myth. It's true that building a culture where people know the organization truly cares about them takes time and energy. But, if companies are not genuine in their desire to build a culture of respect and trust, people will see right through thinly disguised attempts to get them to produce more! Making people feel valued isn't a program that can be implemented and doing so won't create the buy-in that organizations are looking for. Putting a "People are our greatest asset" plaque on the reception room wall won't do it either. Neither will hiring human resources staff and giving them the task of "making people feel valued."

The real win comes not in finding some happy midpoint between the two extremes but in finding the place where staff members know that the organization values them highly as individuals, *and* they're successful in producing with excellence. If it's overdone, and people are treated as though they're extremely important, even though they know that they don't actually produce anything, they feel patronized, not valued! There's no better way we know to show people how valuable they are than to let them be a significant part of an organization that outperforms the competition, is innovative, and has a strong future.

> *Valuing people is not a program the company implements.*

How does an organization communicate value to someone? Primarily, organizations show people they're valuable when they pay attention, listen, and understand their needs. People feel valued when they are allowed to make decisions that *matter* to the organization and are then held accountable for the results.

We also need to communicate that value does not equal output by making sure we communicate with them about much more than just our desires and their performance. We've got to take the time to actually get involved with them. We have to actually know them and respond to their need for relationship. John C. Maxwell, author and leadership guru, says, "You don't really know someone until you know what makes them laugh, what makes them cry, and what makes them dream."[8] If they feel that others are too busy to spend a little time listening to what's important to them, what they hear is that the only thing that matters is what they *do*, not *who they are*.

There's a fly in the ointment—if we work at letting a person know they are important, but they *personally don't feel like they're important*, then they feel patronized instead of valued! So, all of this assumes (and puts sound justification behind the idea) that we have to communicate real information to people. We have to let them know how the company is really doing and if what they're contributing is helping or not. As author and teacher Steven Covey notes, "People are not just resources or assets, not just economic, social, and psychological beings; they are also spiritual beings; they want meaning, a sense of doing something that matters. People do not want to work for a cause with little meaning, even though it taps their mental capacities to the fullest. There must be purposes that lift them, ennoble them, and bring them to their highest selves."[9]

There are things an organization can do to show that it values its staff.

➤ Be sure that staff members have a clear sense how their jobs and tasks fit into the corporate goals and vision. Make sure that there's a way to link one to the other so that people understand, in practical terms, how their efforts actually matter.

➤ Before making any decision that will affect someone, give them a chance to have input into the process and then actually listen to what they have to say. Ask them how their ideas might affect others and help them think beyond the limits of their own job or department. If there are outside factors that they don't know about, fill them in—don't make assumptions about what they know or should know.

➤ If people's input can't be used, make an effort to help them understand why not.

➤ Be sure that all communication is honest, especially bad news. Teach managers and supervisors how to share facts and figures in ways that have practical meaning and relevance. When the news is tough, make sure that people understand exactly what they can expect to happen next.

➤ As much as possible, work at giving people choices: it's one of the most effective ways to bring balance to the Value scale.

Aptitudes and Gifts

Leaders and supervisors in healthy organizations do much more than simply oversee quality and process—they schedule the work and make sure that people are doing what they were hired to do. Once again, we're not proposing a functional nightmare where work doesn't get done because somebody doesn't like doing it. In the short term, the focus needs to be on the specific tasks that have to be completed—leaders juggle priorities and staff to make sure that production and quality are where they need to be. Supervisors don't need to feel any hesitation about asking staff members to do things that aren't necessarily what they do best, as long as they keep in mind that in the longer term, they have an underlying responsibility to move them toward something that *is* a better fit. And, in the short term, leaders apply whatever support is needed to make the process as positive as it can be, given the present reality.

On the staff side, balance requires that employees keep a long-term outlook on their career plans. Life has a way of teaching us that there are always jobs to do that we'd rather not have to handle. To raise a son or daughter that makes us proud, we have to put up with a bunch of jobs we'd rather not have to handle—everything from changing diapers to paying for college! It's the promise of the future that keeps us actively engaged in something that we don't entirely enjoy now. Most adults understand they have to be willing to do what's *necessary* on the road to doing what they *love*; most people recognize that as a reasonable trade-off.

Whether organizations make some sort of commitment toward helping employees achieve career goals or not isn't the primary indicator of health. Organizations don't need to accept responsibility for helping staff actually achieve career goals. The big difference between healthy organizations and less robust ones is that healthy organizations have a track record of success that they can point to in terms of moving staff into positions where they are able to use their gifts, maximizing their strengths and minimizing the exposure of their weaknesses. When there isn't a solid track record, employees tend to get pessimistic about the future and complain about the work they're asked to do. When the track record is there, employees are more willing to adapt their own plans to fit the realities of the job. Because they're being given the opportunity to leverage their strengths, they recast their career goals in light of their experiences in their present positions, instead of feeling like they need to move to a different organization to get the opportunities they dream about.

> "Don't ask yourself what the world needs; ask yourself what makes you come alive. And then go and do that. Because what the world needs is people who have come alive."
>
> —Howard Thurman

Healthy organizations avoid the extremes, reaching widely in terms of gifts and abilities. Part of finding a range of balance is in being willing to confront someone who isn't pulling their weight. The balance point isn't at the center of the spectrum, where employees have to tolerate a bit of control from leaders but can at least assume they won't be overly corrected either. It's hard to imagine how an environment like that would work! Healthy organizations find balance by doing their best to align the primary assignments for staff with their gifts as best as they're able to understand them *and* by making sure that the culture is based on doing what it takes to turn out excellence. They encourage staff to work toward positions that play to their strengths *and* reward those who do what's necessary to ensure that the whole team wins, even when it's not part of their strong suit.

All of this presumes that an organization can define and measure a person's gifts and has a way of categorizing them and cross-referencing them to roles or job descriptions. An organization that has a strong desire to respect gifts and strengths but has no way to identify which gift is required for which role is no closer to being healthy than an organization that ignores the area of gifts and abilities altogether. Within a team, it's important that various team members understand each other's gifts and know how each member's strengths can be applied to the tasks at hand. Team cohesiveness is based on knowing each other's strengths and weaknesses and holding each other accountable for behaviors and actions in light of that knowledge.[10]

Here's what an organization can do to a place of balance on the Aptitude value scale:

➢ Know how to measure aptitudes, using tools like the DISC personality profile, the Meyers-Briggs Type Indicator (MBTI), our WRI tool (see Chapter 10), and other profiling systems or skills tests.

➢ Have a way of identifying which employees need to complete profiles and a way of filing and referencing completed profiles.

➢ Know what strengths are needed for a given role and not only match candidates' strengths to the role, but also know where to find existing staff who may be reassigned to that role based on their strength profiles.

➢ Staff members in healthy organizations know how to communicate with co-workers in terms of describing strengths and weaknesses, using terminology that everyone understands and benchmarks that everyone knows.

➢ Supervisors in healthy organizations are taught how to combine the strengths and gifts of various team members to achieve synergies and know how to hold staff members accountable for their performance in the areas where strengths and gifts exist.

➤ Managers in healthy organizations study employees and let the reactions of co-workers influence the recognition of a person's gifts. Who is the go-to person for problems, for example? Often, it's the person with a gift, irrespective of their formal training.

Learning and Growth

There's no doubt that it's important to encourage staff members to get better at what they already do, providing the support, encouragement, and sometimes even the motivation to help them learn what it takes to move up a step in terms of responsibility or influence. Healthy organizations know that effective growth goes well beyond the job to aspects of character, habits, strengths, and weaknesses. Healthy organizations help people to understand that there isn't a clean break between the two—who they are in life includes who they are at the workplace.

Healthy organizations find ways to encourage employees to develop as *people*, not just as *staff members*. They reach outside the workplace into families and communities, knowing that anything they can do to help their staff in those environments will inevitably make a positive impact at work.

Finding the healthy balance on this scale requires vision. Companies that are successful in business have vision statements to tell them where they'd like to be in the future. Organizations that inspire employees to grow help them develop a vision for their lives—a picture of what the future could look like—and a workable plan to help them get there. Healthy organizations help their people build what would have to be called a Life Plan more than a career plan. Finding the balance has less to do with *how* organizations see growth as it does with the scope at which they expect and support it.

It might seem that there's a reasonable case to be made here for a point of balance that is more or less in the middle of the scale, where the company is neither indifferent nor manipulative about growth. In the first two values, we found that the scale balances best when it's set on as wide a foundation as possible and that certainly applies here as well. It's been our experience, however, that organizations need to deliberately embrace a bit more of the right side of the learning value scale. Why? There are two reasons.

First, indifference is surprisingly easy to communicate. As we mentioned before, to let someone know that you really don't care, you simply do *nothing*. In practical terms, that means that it's exceptionally easy to live along the left-ditch of the road!

Second, manipulation (the other extreme) is surprisingly easy to avoid. There are a couple of boundaries that healthy organizations won't cross because it would mean moving into the manipulation ditch. The message these healthy organizations send to their staff members is:

1. We care about whether you grow or not, but we're not going to accept the *responsibility* for your growth.

2. We *will* hold you accountable for the choices you're making. You can't just take a program as a way of ducking out on the consequences of your attitudes or character flaws.

There's an important distinction between helping someone grow, and taking responsibility for their growth. We're not accepting responsibility for a person's growth when we measure the outcome of a program—programs should be expected to produce results. We cross the line when we take responsibility for whether or not they actually *apply* what they've learned or whether it brings noticeable change to their lives. However, just because we don't take responsibility for the outcome doesn't mean that we can't continue to insist that staff members learn to fit in with the culture we've created or live with the consequences if they can't or won't.

There's one other important limit in place in healthy organizations. They don't violate the first value to make Learning and Growth work: they don't devalue people who don't want to participate, While there might be consequences for choosing not to participate—an employee might not qualify for a promotion, for example—it won't mean that they're disrespected or ridiculed. If someone doesn't want to deal with a character flaw your way, they're not written off. There isn't an assumption that because they aren't dealing with the problem, somehow they are "stupid" or "lazy." The reality may be that the person *can't* deal with it, not that they *won't*.

To bring balance to the Learning and Growth value:

➤ Let staff members know that you care about what they're good at and what they're interested in. Give them the freedom to apply for internal transfers when opportunities come up in an area they think they would do well at.

➤ Provide access to programs that help staff grow in terms of areas that are of interest to them and have a positive impact on the organization as well. For example:

1. Offering courses about managing their investments is usually seen as being of high value to staff members. The benefit to the company is that staff who take the courses also learn how to handle the company's resources more effectively.

2. Offering courses about communication skills helps staff members in many areas of life. Staff members who learn to communicate better at home or with friends are also going to apply that knowledge to their communication at work.

➤ Provide education credits that allow staff to access low-interest loans for courses they take at recognized educational institutions. Don't worry about what they take—if they do well, give them access to the funding. The fact that they put themselves into a learning mindset is a significant benefit to the organization.

➢ For supervisors, teach internal courses that focus on the culture of the organization and how it differs from other organizations where they may have learned supervision skills. Help them understand their role in maintaining the culture that the organization has spent time and effort developing.

➢ Offer lots of courses and short seminars (perhaps even on paid time) that help staff members use time management tools, learn to keep proper files and records, improve their technical skills, and so on. Give a gifted employee a few extra hours to prepare a seminar and do the teaching—that's who others go to when they have questions anyway!

Make sure that you have a strong growth-oriented culture in the organization. Courses, seminars, and training sessions should be a normal and welcome part of the routine, not a disruptive annoyance that people do their best to avoid.

Unity in Community

For the most part, all of us want to have healthy cultures in our workplaces. Just what that means may vary from person to person, but almost everyone understands that a fun and relationally rewarding environment is preferable to a mundane and boring one. It's certainly preferable to a toxic, cynical, and conflict-filled workplace! What may not be understood is that to have a fun and relationally rewarding environment, it has to be designed and built *on purpose*. A great corporate culture that creates unity and community doesn't happen by chance—it happens when we take the time and invest the effort to define the culture we want and then take active steps to implement and maintain it.

Books about organizations that are great places to work don't start out with statements like, "What we wanted to build was an incredibly efficient money-making venture that would produce enormous profits for shareholders." There are undoubtedly organizations like that, but they're not the healthy organization success stories—the places where people absolutely love to work. Those stories usually start with statements that talk about the *kind of place* it was going to be, the *kind of people* they wanted to employ, and the *culture* they were going to embrace. Culture was designed on purpose, not left to form by default. That's not to suggest that profitability wasn't one of the goals—there's nothing unhealthy about producing a good return on the shareholder's investment. When businesses aren't profitable, they don't keep running, no matter how great the culture may be! Remember that our definition of a healthy organization says that it must be productive as well as being a place where respect, trust, and service flourish.

Healthy organizations must be productive as well as respectful, trusting, and service-oriented.

One of the ways that organizations communicate their cultural expectations to staff members is through the policies and procedures manual. Even in small organizations where the policies aren't formally written down, they are still communicated pretty clearly by the attitudes and actions of owners or leaders. Avoid communicating to people that they aren't trusted to do the right things and that the organization is putting all sorts of measures into place to ensure that nobody can get more than their fair share. Doing this fosters dissent. Instead, it needs to be clear that respect and trust will characterize the relationship between leaders, staff members, customers and clients, and everyone else who comes into contact with the organization. Deal with breaches of trust as issues of character, outside of policy.

The Unity value system measures how people protect their own interests and how they make sacrifices for each other—how they show understanding and flexibility. That's why it's so important that policies and expectations are communicated in a way that says, "We have certain expectations, and we think that they're reasonable. We do understand that there are sometimes extenuating circumstances, and so we want to be flexible about how the policies are applied." The way to do that is to be clear about the principles behind the policies—the ideology or philosophy that drives them.

When an organization wants to make sure that they communicate policies in a healthy way, they need to step back and think about *why* the policy exists—what are the *principles* that it's built to communicate and protect?

If you want a culture of respect, trust, and service, then those are the principles that have to underscore each and every policy in the organization. When leaders write policies, they have to go back to those principles over and over. They have to keep asking questions like:

> ➢ Is this policy respectful of the organization's *and* the staff member's needs? Can supervisors and managers apply it fairly and reasonably?

> ➢ Is the policy written from the perspective that the people it applies to are trustworthy—that they want to do the *right things*, and need to know what those right things are? (Typical policies are written to prevent people from doing the *wrong things*.)

> ➢ Is the policy written in ways that direct managers, supervisors, and other leaders to *serve* the people they lead? In other words, does the policy equip leaders to help other staff members live out the principles of respect and trust toward each other as well as toward clients, customers, suppliers, and others who are outside the organization?

Will there be people who see this as an opportunity to take unfair advantage of the organization? Undoubtedly. There are always a few people who live in the left-ditch personally and care only about what happens to them. We don't deny that they exist, and we don't deny any organization the right to protect themselves from that sort of abuse. Our argument however, is that using a *policy* to attempt to prevent people like that from acting as they do is misguided. What that does is create two problems. First, it makes everyone feel that they're all suspected of having such motives—which is clearly unwise. Second, it betrays an unwillingness on the organization's part to invest the time and energy required to confront the few people who have wrong motives and encourage them to change their ways or pack their bags and leave.

It's very easy to wander off balance on this value. It seems a lot easier to simply bang down the gavel and pass a "law" than it is to craft principle-centered policies. It seems easier to write a policy that specifies "just cause for dismissal" and then fire someone over a violation than it is to specify "expected behavior" and work with the staff members who don't measure up, until they either change or make it clear that they can't or won't change. We're not convinced that's true. In organizations where policies are written from the perspective we prescribe, the policy manuals tend to be fairly small and easy to understand. When policies are written to carefully close every possible loophole, the manuals can be enormous. When new staff members can take the whole policy manual home and read it in an evening, there's a good chance you can expect them to understand it and use it to guide the way they behave and interact at work. When the manual is several hundred pages long, and they need a lawyer to explain it to them, you can hardly expect them to feel trusted and respected. (If they can't understand it, how can they act according to your expectations?)

What about the legal position such policies might leave an organization in? We're not suggesting that organizations get rid of their attorneys and legal departments. Staff members that need to be moved out of the organization may sue when they're dismissed, and the organization has every right to protect itself and the healthier employees from abuse. That's all part of finding the balance on Unity value scale.

What if you work in an organization that already has a tightly defined set of rules, designed around the idea that people are going to try and cheat the system and get something they're not entitled to? What do you do then? How do you start adjusting things so that there's a clear shift in communication toward trusting, respectful relationships in the workplace?

➢ Start by defining the principles that you want as a foundation for your culture.

➢ Revisit the policies, one at a time, and rework them so they fit within the principles you've defined. Do that with lots of consultation with staff members, supervisors, and legal counsel but stay true to the principles.

➢ Find ways to assess or measure the culture that's in the organization now. (We dedicate Chapter 8 to that exercise.) Find the silos where toxicity exists and work hard to rebuild the culture there.

➢ Develop a conflict resolution process and implement it across the organization.

Building a warm, supportive, and engaging culture in the workplace is well worth the effort that it takes. After the culture is assessed, you can start to build what you envision.

Empathy and Generosity

Have you ever smashed your thumb with a hammer? What's the first thing you do? Do you instantly look at your thumb and think, "What were you doing there? You had no business being there—you deserved to get hit!" Not likely! The *first* thing most of us would do is and grab the thumb with the other hand. Then, after a few seconds, suck in a deep breath and take a closer look at the damage to decide if things are okay or if this is going to need a trip to the emergency room. The self talk comes later—the analysis of why and how it got hurt and what should be done to prevent a similar accident in the future.

In healthy organizations, the reaction to a crisis in the life of an employee looks a lot like that. There's an immediate response—an almost automatic reaction—to come alongside the person who has a need and offer support and comfort. The first reaction is to help as much as possible to deal with the immediate need. Then, once the situation is under control, they begin asking questions about longer term care and eventually, about prevention.

As we see it, there are four loosely defined milestones along the process of responding to a crisis in a healthy organization:

1. Immediate care that isn't primarily concerned about cost or convenience. The focus is on providing tangible support.

2. Begin to assess the damage and get some sense of what sort of plan needs to be put into place to make sure that healing or recovery is possible and takes place as quickly as is reasonable.

3. Develop a plan for long-term care and rehabilitation.

4. Do the analysis designed to prevent recurrence or further problems and then implement the changes or safeguards that are necessary.

In other words, healthy organizations find a wide range over which they balance this value. They want both generosity *and* accountability, in a healthy balance with each other. That can create some tension, but as long as the organization makes it a principle to *respond first* and ask the questions later, the tension can be worked out in a healthy way.

The first two steps in the process above (immediate care and then an assessment of the damage) need to be done almost without any sort of accountability at all. The focus is on providing tangible and helpful support to the person with a need. Only as the second step begins to give way to the third does the discussion of accountability even *begin* to enter the process. And, only as part of the fourth step does accountability actually become an important part of the discussion.

It's not as simple as it sounds. When we injure a thumb, we don't have to wonder who's responsible to provide support. We don't have to think about budgets and approvals. And, we don't have to think about how to detect the pain in the first place—our nervous systems do that automatically. Having a healthy organization doesn't simply mean that there's a policy somewhere to declare that offering immediate support is duly authorized. To be healthy, an organization has to find ways to *detect* that someone has a need. It's the detection mechanism that triggers the support system. No one knows what's going on in the lives of nameless individuals who are only known by their employee number. Supervisors and leaders all the way up the chain of command need to be relationally connected to the teams they lead. They need to know enough about each person to know when there's a problem and what kind of help would be appreciated and actually be *helpful*.

Beyond that level of relational connection, supervisors and leaders have to know *ahead of time* that there are discretionary budgets available for providing the immediate care that's needed. In most cases, the cost of immediate care is reasonable. Most of the time, it involves letting an employee take an extra day or two off work. Often, the situation revolves around finding the time to tend to something unpredictable but not long-term—a child or a spouse is unexpectedly ill or a child-care arrangement falls through. There are, of course, situations where there's a crisis—a death in the family or a medical emergency for example—but even in those situations, an extra day or two can make a significant difference.

Sometimes the right response is to offer the employee access to corporate facilities in a creative way—giving an employee priority access to the corporate travel department to arrange a trip on short notice, for example. It might be as simple as giving an employee the keys to a company vehicle to pick up a sick child from school and a few minutes to arrange for care at a friend or relative's home.

Once the initial situation is handled through the first two steps, there needs to be a deliberate move to the third step. What else needs to be done so that the situation can return to normal? Will further help be necessary? Will the response require escalation to someone with more authority?

Situations where the problem is more chronic than acute—issues related to stress, burnout, or other soft injury—aren't easily solved by a few days off or the keys to a company car. Remember though, in healthy organizations, these soft injuries are already reduced because staff who are valued and working in areas where they have natural gifts are being supported as they grow and face challenges and know the organization stands behind them. They are *much less likely* to experience negative job stress or burnout. As well, supervisors and leaders who are connected relationally to staff are in a very good position to notice job stress building up long before it becomes a chronic problem. That's not to suggest that burnout never happens in healthy organizations. It's just that when it does, the company already has a culture in place that provides immediate relief, has a way of planning for effective care and rehabilitation, and then starts talking with the employee about how they will work together to make sure that the problem doesn't reoccur.

Organizations that are out of balance toward the left end of the scale introduce accountability as part of the process *too early*. By trying to deal with who is responsible for the situation while there's still a need for immediate care (Step 1), they send the message that they don't really care about an employee's pain as much as they care about their own loss of productivity or income or the cost of offering help. While it's likely oversimplifying a complex issue, there are some reasons that unhealthy organizations tend to respond on the left of the scale. The first is that leaders act out of fear or concern that if they become involved, they will somehow inherit liability or responsibility for a situation that they would rather distance themselves from. In some cases, that translates into a concern that they may become enablers of people who want to take unfair advantage of their generosity. The other possibility is that they're simply callous and don't care. (Leaders who are relationally connected to staff so poorly that they can't tell when there's a need fall into this category.)

Fear that the organization will somehow inherit liability if it becomes involved is likely a moot point. If the organization has contributed to the crisis in some way, then it's already involved, and offering help becomes a *moral* responsibility. If the organization is offering help in a situation where they clearly have no involvement in its cause, it would be difficult to imagine a scenario where their help would be construed as inappropriate or as creating legal liability.

In terms of enabling "freeloaders," we suggest that if there are freeloaders in the organization (which there may very well be), then they are going to take unfair advantage of the company whether the company is generous or not. Furthermore, denying them access to generous and charitable assistance programs is not the way to try and control the problem. Holding them accountable for their attitudes and actions *before* there's a crisis is a much better solution. Blaming a generous assistance program for enabling their poor attitude is a misplaced judgment that unfairly penalizes those who need the support systems.

Chapter 8:   Organizational Checkup

Organizational dysfunction happens when there's a disconnect between what people *expect* and what they *get*. It has little or nothing to do with what's advertised or promised. If an organization tells potential hires, "We pay well, but this place is terrible to work for—you're going to be mistreated, used, and discarded like some old rag when we're done with you," employees would still complain when they were mistreated, used, and discarded. Knowing mistreatment is likely doesn't make it any more palatable when it happens! The point is, it's not the gap between what an organization *says* and what it *does* that causes the problem; it's the mismatch between *what the organization does* and what *employees think they should do* that causes the dysfunction, In other words, how employees think in terms of the five value systems just doesn't match the way that the organization acts.

So how do we measure organizational dysfunction? How do we identify and quantify it so that we can put specific plans into place that are intended to treat it? That can be difficult. It's a bit like diagnosing a medical condition.

Suppose someone tells you, "I have a headache. What's causing it? Any ideas?" Without having a lot more information, you really have no idea what's causing it. The cause could be as simple as caffeine withdrawal, a poor night's sleep, or a posture problem. It could also be as serious as a brain tumor. The point is that one or two symptoms in themselves don't describe a condition very well. What you need in order to make a good diagnosis, are predictable groups of symptoms—there need to be enough of them, and they need to fit a pattern well.

The same thing is true in an organization. One or two employees who are unhappy among a majority that report high satisfaction levels don't describe an organization that's unhealthy. But, if we find groups of employees that feel disappointed or unhappy about a consistent set of issues, we're probably onto something significant.

What we have to do is measure two different things. First, we need to measure how well staff members respond to the organization's culture. How satisfied are they with the status quo? Do they feel that they're valued, well placed, encouraged to grow, happy with the demands and challenges of their work, and well supported? (We're about to introduce a tool, the Organizational Health Survey, which will help to measure this.)

Second, we need to get a sense of where the leaders that set the culture have their personal value systems. We need to know that because it's very likely that their personal value systems are going to set the tone for the values that the organization reflects.

Organizational Health Survey

The best way we know to give employees a chance to identify their perceptions—their analysis—of the health of the organization that they work for is to ask them in a format where their answers are kept confidential. We've divided the survey into sections that assess the values we've identified earlier—Value, Aptitude, Learning, Unity, and Empathy (V.A.L.U.E.).

We ask people to score the survey based on a simple scale of 1 (strongly disagree) to 5 (strongly agree). They pick a number in the middle if their sentiment falls between the two.

You're welcome to use the questions we present here as part of your own survey. If you prefer, you can create your own set of questions:

Value

Disagree Agree	We believe that people have inherent value that goes beyond their ability to produce or to please.
1 2 3 4 5	1. Supervisors, managers, and owners of our organization demonstrate by their actions that they attach high importance to people.
1 2 3 4 5	2. The leaders of our organization demonstrate trust in the staff.
1 2 3 4 5	3. Our organization invests in those who work or volunteer here.
1 2 3 4 5	4. The overall approach of our leaders builds loyalty in the staff of our organization.
1 2 3 4 5	5. I can think of at least one thing I've seen our organization do in the last three months that really served one of the workers.
1 2 3 4 5	6. The co-workers in our organization have a good reputation for respecting one another.
1 2 3 4 5	7. Our organization does a good job of balancing people's needs with the bottom line.

Very low scores (the average is less than 2) indicate that there are problems with respect and trust; staff perceive that the focus is almost exclusively on the value of their work rather than their value as a person. Moderate scores, between 2 and 4, indicate that staff members feel somewhat valued and appreciated, but there's room for growth. High scores (the average is above 4) indicate that employees feel highly valued, and value-related dysfunction is not likely to exist.

Aptitude

Disagree	Agree	We believe that people's gifts and abilities are an essential part of who they are and what they were destined to do.
1 2 3 4 5		8. In our organization it's clear that the leadership team values people's unique gifts, talents, and abilities.
1 2 3 4 5		9. There are deliberate steps taken by our organization to help people find the right place to work within our organization.
1 2 3 4 5		10. People in our organization seem to have a fair bit of passion for doing their responsibilities well.
1 2 3 4 5		11. I enjoy the responsibilities that I have in my organization.
1 2 3 4 5		12. Leaders and supervisors seem interested in helping staff move into responsibilities that best suit them.
1 2 3 4 5		13. Leaders and supervisors have the courage to move people out of responsibilities when they are not performing them well.
1 2 3 4 5		14. I am clear on how I can use my gifts and abilities to make the best contribution possible to my organization.

Very low scores (the average is less than 2) indicate that staff perceive an overly directive environment in the workplace. Moderate scores, between 2 and 4, indicate that staff members feel management is generally supportive and helpful. High scores (the average is above 4) indicate that employees feel a high level of satisfaction with their work, and their roles are well matched to their gifts and aptitudes.

Learning

Disagree		Agree	We believe that people need to grow if they are to succeed and experience the rewards of that success.
1 2 3 4 5			15. Our organization provides resources to support individuals in reaching their professional development goals.
1 2 3 4 5			16. Our organization recognizes the value of personal and professional development and provides opportunities for this.
1 2 3 4 5			17. I have the opportunity to receive the training that I need to fulfill my responsibilities.
1 2 3 4 5			18. I work with people who are open to correction and show a willingness to develop in areas of weakness.
1 2 3 4 5			19. The organization's environment permits open and candid communication.
1 2 3 4 5			20. The staff in our organization have taken steps in the past year to improve their skills.
1 2 3 4 5			21. Our organization gains more clients each year without losing an unhealthy number of our current clients.

Very low scores (the average is less than 2) indicate that there are problems with perceived indifference and employees feel that leaders see individual goals for growth and development as irrelevant. It could indicate there are problems with a manipulative view of growth plans because employees feel forced to take courses that seem irrelevant. (A simple review of the organization's actions will quickly tell which extreme is to blame.) Moderate scores, between 2 and 4, indicate that staff members feel their goals and aspirations are at least considered. High scores (the average is above 4) indicate that employees feel confident of the organization's support for their growth plans.

Unity

Disagree ⟶ Agree	We believe that people need a nurturing, trusting, and fun place to belong to, where they can relate to their peers.
1 2 3 4 5	22. We visibly respect others and hear the opinions of others even if one does not personally hold the same opinion.
1 2 3 4 5	23. I would recommend our organization as one of the best places to work in our community.
1 2 3 4 5	24. I work with people who demonstrate maturity in character.
1 2 3 4 5	25. Our organization is a fun place to work.
1 2 3 4 5	26. The policies of our organization are reasonable and fair.
1 2 3 4 5	27. The level of internal communications in our organization, both written and verbal, meets my needs.
1 2 3 4 5	28. I enjoy the people I work with.

Very low scores (the average is less than 2) indicate that there are problems with a sense of community and camaraderie in the workplace. Moderate scores, between 2 and 4, indicate that staff members feel as though they belong to a supportive community. High scores (the average is above 4) indicate that employees thoroughly enjoy the work environment and feel positive about their co-workers.

Empathy

Disagree Agree	*We believe people need support to help them get through challenging times.*
1 2 3 4 5	29. Our organization shows empathy toward staff by acting in a caring, kind, and understanding manner when someone on our staff is facing a difficult life situation.
1 2 3 4 5	30. Our organization has practices in place that support me in maintaining work/life balance.
1 2 3 4 5	31. I receive support from our organization for personal issues when I am in need.
1 2 3 4 5	32. I can recall at least one time in the past three months when someone in our organization reached out to support a fellow staff member.
1 2 3 4 5	33. Absenteeism is not a problem in our organization.
1 2 3 4 5	34. Our organization has practices in place to allow staff flexibility in scheduling their work.
1 2 3 4 5	35. The leaders in our organization know and value that each person has a life away from the organization.

Very low scores (the average is less than 2) indicate that employees don't feel that support will be available when they need it. Moderate scores, between 2 and 4, indicate that staff members feel that help will be available to some degree. High scores (the average is above 4) show that staff feel support is available, appropriate, and making a difference.

Interpreting Results

We freely admit that the survey is a subjective measurement tool, but it's our opinion that measuring satisfaction is inherently subjective anyway. The survey gives a clear, accurate reading about how healthy the organization is when it's completed by the entire staff. Because the questions tie directly into the five values, the results indicate how well the organization expresses in *helpful, practical ways* its commitment to the values that it holds. The survey is going to reveal very practical things about the culture of the organization and the way that employees see the company supporting them and responding to their needs and preferences.

We also admit that our own bias is built into the survey—it reflects a somewhat right-leaning value preference. We understand that doesn't necessarily reflect the point of view taken by every organization's leadership. There are two reasons for the bias.

First, while organizations have the right to choose how they build their culture and where they establish the balance on the value scales, historically the bias has been well to the left, in favor of budgets, rules, performance, and accountability. The survey presumes that some weight needs to be added to the right side of the scale to achieve balance. Most organizations already know how to measure financial performance, customer satisfaction, and process improvement (three of the four quadrants of the Balanced Scorecard.[11]) Using the survey as it stands to address the fourth Learning and Growth quadrant allows them to add counterweight to those three left-leaning quadrants.

The second reason is related to people's perceptions. Whether the organization's balance is biased somewhat to the left, right, or nearer the center, employee satisfaction will be highest when employees share the organization's bias. When personal and organizational value systems match, employees score the survey favorably. When the values mismatch, the opposite happens.

Self-aware Leaders

Having leaders assess themselves can reveal where they rests on the value scales. The value systems that the leaders of an organization hold to personally are usually the values that are reflected in the corporate culture. If leaders tend to lean to the left or right in their thinking, then the culture of the organization tends to lean similarly left or right.

The self-assessment below simply asks you to pick a number on a scale. Negative numbers take you toward the left and positive numbers toward the right for each of the five value systems. Zero lies in the center of the scale. Now that you understand the value systems and how they work, you should be able to do the self-assessment without any trouble. Do you tend to lean one way or the other?

VALUE					
Slave Driver -5	-4 -3 -2	-1 0 1	2 3 4	5	*People-Pleaser*
Task-Oriented					People-Oriented
APTITUDE					
Just Get It Done -5	-4 -3 -2	-1 0 1	2 3 4	5	*Soft Touch*
Directive					Permissive
LEARNING					*We Know What's*
On Your Own Dime -5	-4 -3 -2	-1 0 1	2 3 4	5	*Best For You*
Indifference					Manipulative
UNITY					
Look Out For #1 -5	-4 -3 -2	-1 0 1	2 3 4	5	*Yes-Man*
Personal					Corporate
EMPATHY					
Hard-Liner -5	-4 -3 -2	-1 0 1	2 3 4	5	*Bleeding Heart*
Accountability					Charity

The Cost of Balance

Whether they realize it or not, the leaders who make the financial decisions and define the practices that set the culture in place are affecting the organization by deciding what it can afford to spend on its people.

Their own personal value systems, combined with their willingness to put time, money, and other resources behind those value systems, have a strong influence on the culture that forms around them.

Decisions to live at any point along the value system have human and financial costs. There are no "free spots" along the scales. As organizations move to the left, away from the "softer" side where people's wants, likes, and dislikes have a higher priority, they reduce the immediate financial costs. That doesn't necessarily mean that a move to the left is automatically better for the bottom line—it means that direct HR costs go down somewhat, but there is an increased "human cost" to pay. As they move to the right, the opposite happens: HR costs go up somewhat, and the priority shifts slightly toward the softer "people issues" and away from the harder financial issues.

There are no "free" spots along the scales.

Don't assume that somehow living near the center is cheaper or free. There's no formula that identifies the cheapest spot on the spectrum. It's a question of health. If the organization is consistent and the values that the organization holds to and the values that the staff expects are the same, then the company is healthy—whether it leans left, sits near the center, or leans right. Extreme points of view (in-the-ditch thinking about the values) or inconsistency foster disagreement about what's acceptable and what's not, and the likelihood of finding organizational dysfunction goes up dramatically. Addressing the problems and pain points that result from dysfunction makes *both* financial cost *and* human cost go down, and makes *both* employee satisfaction *and* the bottom line go up.

Chapter 9:   Measuring Personal Values

The WRI (Workplace Relationship Indicator) Instrument

In the next chapter, we're going to look at what happens when two people feel differently about their preferred values and what happens when there's inconsistency within one person's value systems. Before we can do that with any sort of accuracy, we need a way of establishing which way a person leans on their values: left, center, or right.

The WRI, or the Workplace Relationship Indicator, is a testing instrument that helps you identify your biases on each of the five values. (A full version of the instrument is available from www.bhogroup.com.) We've included a simplified version, a 60-question, "forced choice" instrument below.

How you answer the questions is up to you, and there's no reason why you can't go back and change your answers over time. In fact, if you get to the end of the instrument, and you don't like a strong left-leaning or right-leaning score, just go back and look at the questions again and change them if you feel that you can do so honestly. The instrument is designed to help you sort out your own biases and provide a way of embracing the paradox and moving to a balanced position, It's not intended to pigeon-hole you into an assessment that feels unfair.

For each pair of questions, select either the A or the B answer. If you're not sure, go with the one that reflects how you usually act.

Value

1.	A. I like to find people who help me get things done. B. I enjoy working with most people.
2.	A. I prefer working with people who focus on their tasks. B. I like relating with people at work.
3.	A. I make an effort to explain tasks and goals to others. B. I make an effort to understand people.
4.	A. Working with a team often complicates things. B. Working on my own is not very fulfilling.
5.	A. I think people who miss steps in a process are careless. B. I don't think we always need to follow the procedure.
6.	A. People who are social don't usually get results. B. Task-oriented people are too driven for me.

Aptitude

1.	A. People need to do the jobs they are assigned. B. People need to do what they enjoy doing.
2.	A. Everyone working on the team should do an equal share. B. Each person on the team contributes something unique.
3.	A. I like to get everyone busy on reaching the goal. B. I like to understand what motivates a person.
4.	A. I confront people who miss deadlines or do poor work. B. I help people find work they have passion for.
5.	A. I like handing out jobs for people to do. B. I don't like telling people what to do.
6.	A. I can't make others feel happy and fulfilled. B. I try to keep other people's work exciting.

Learning

1.	A. I take people at face value—they are who they are. B. I can usually see potential in people.
2.	A. I like to teach people the skills they need for their job. B. I like to inspire people to try new things.
3.	A. I try to avoid people with personal issues. B. I try to help people learn new ways of relating.
4.	A. It's not my job to help others follow their career plans. B. I like to see others promoted to higher responsibility.

5.	A. I feel threatened when someone tries to learn my job.
	B. If I teach others my job, I can try something new.
6.	A. I expect excellence from my team.
	B. I have a strong sense of what people would be good at.

Unity

1.	A. I don't mind working hard, but I have my own life to live.
	B. There's little time for my own needs after work, friends, and family.
2.	A. I feel that work should come before play.
	B. I like making the work environment fun.
3.	A. I like the structure of having clear rules and policies.
	B. I like the flexibility to adjust policies when necessary.
4.	A. I do a good job even when others don't.
	B. I like to find ways to help other people do well.
5.	A. Keeping to myself helps me stay focused.
	B. I appreciate lots of interaction with others.
6.	A. I try to keep problems at home and at work separate.
	B. Problems in one part of life tend to affect other areas.

Empathy

1.	A. I only help when I see how it will make a difference.
	B. Helping is making a difference.
2.	A. I'd rather help someone understand their problem than treat symptoms.
	B. I am good at helping people get through their immediate needs.
3.	A. I try to solve problems for myself before I ask for help.
	B. I am quick to ask for help when I have a need.
4.	A. I have expectations about how my help should be used.
	B. I tend not to think about whether someone will take advantage of me.
5.	A. I value strategy, planning, and patience in providing support and care.
	B. I value sensitive, quick responses to supporting others in need.
6.	A. People need to acknowledge that they create many of their own problems.
	B. There are a lot of things that people can't easily control.

Scoring:

	Number of B Choices	Number of A Choices	Subtract B from A for your score:
Value			
Aptitude			
Learning			
Unity			
Empathy			

Scores for each value system will range from -6 (zero B scores minus six A scores) to +6 (six B scores minus zero A scores).

Interpreting Your Scores

Scores less than zero are left-leaning scores, and scores greater than zero lean to the right. The further to the left the average of your scores on the five value scales are, the more likely that you are to prioritize the concrete aspects of the workplace (the activities or tasks) and the more likely you are to expect others to simply do what you ask of them. The further right your average score is, the more likely you are to prioritize the abstract aspects of the workplace (fulfillment or enjoyment), and the more likely you are to expect others to focus on relating to each other.

Significant Left Scores

If your score is -4 or -6, you have strong left-leaning thinking patterns in that value scale. When our internal value systems lean strongly left, we dramatically increase the likelihood that others will find relating to us quite difficult. Taking a more balanced position may help you to build the trust that is necessary for healthy workplace relationships.

Center Scores

Scores between -2 and +2 are mid-range scores. These scores indicate that your personal values fall into the center zone for workplace relationships. You may have an easier time understanding the positions of others in the workplace than people with significant left or right scores.

Moderate Right Scores

A score of +4 is not as challenging to workplace relationships as the more right-leaning score is. As long as the people you work with are also right-leaning, you will probably find that the workplace stays healthy. If you have to work with others who have scores on the left side of the scale, we predict that over time you will experience significant relational tension in the workplace.

Significant Right Scores

If you have a score of +6, you have strong right-leaning values in that area. When our internal value systems lean strongly right, we increase the likelihood that others will find relating to us difficult. Taking a more balanced position may help you to build the trust that is necessary for healthy workplace relationships.

We include the -4 score in the "significant" category, but we put the +4 score as in its own "moderate" category. That's because the moderate right score (+4) isn't as problematic for workplace relationships as the equivalent left score is. People with right-leaning values tend to be more sensitive toward the "people issues" that cause relational tension in the workplace. They can often avoid conflict by virtue of their focus on people over tasks.

Working With Your Opposite

One of the ways that knowing you WRI score can help you create balance in your thinking is when you work with someone who thinks opposite to you. When we mentor leaders, we encourage them to find someone they respect and trust who has a score opposite theirs. Then we have them work directly with that other person to discuss perceptions and solicit their input on decisions that have to be made. By deliberately looking for an opposite point of view, you demonstrate that you genuinely value the opinion of someone whose perspective is opposite your own. We present more about this in the following chapters.

Don't presume that we're suggesting a moderate or significant score is wrong. Our worldviews—our systems of thinking—often lead us to adopt a right-leaning or left-leaning perspective along one or more of the value scales. We aren't necessarily suggesting that you include the opposite perspective in your decision making so that you will change how you think. (In some circumstances, it's possible that your thinking *will* change over time, but that isn't the point of the exercise.) We're suggesting that broadening your perspective will help you to ensure that you have considered the balancing opinion before you make decisions.

Chapter 10: Value System Alignment

The concept of value system alignment is straightforward. When two people need to work together, the more their value systems align (or, the more overlap between the ranges that they personally are able to embrace), the more likely it is that they will instinctively agree on how things ought to be done. It's not an all or nothing relationship but more of a sliding scale. How the misalignment plays out in the real world has a lot of different factors. People can go from mild disagreement over one of the values to completely opposite opinions about an issue.

It's fairly easy to predict how the disagreement will play out based on which value systems don't align. For example, on the scale of Personal Worth, remember that at one end of the scale there's a sense that accomplishing a goal is more important that worrying about people's feelings. At the other end of the scale, there's a sense that making sure everyone is content is more important than keeping strictly to the schedule. The conflict isn't hard to predict if two people who have to work together but see life from widely differing points along that value system. One will accuse the other of being pushy about goals and schedules and running roughshod over people; the other will feel that the first one doesn't care about progress and that people should just toughen up and get the job done. The greater the gap between the two people, the more intense the feelings will be.

The wider the gap, the more intense the feelings will be.

The presence of a gap is not always negative. There will be times that gaps can be constructive. The next section of the book, where we deal with implementing a healthy value system, talks about how to use the gaps to shift an unhealthy culture; to do what we call a DNA Transplant.

For example, one of our clients is a fairly right-leaning company that struggled for years to be anything more than marginally profitable. Everything else in the company was healthy: staff loved working there, felt highly valued, and agreed that there was lots of opportunity to grow. But, it didn't seem to matter how hard they tried to stay profitable; there was always some limiting factor to their performance on the profit side of the equation. The CEO made a choice to add two senior managers to the management team. Both of them had personal value systems that were slightly left of center on two of the five values. Without compromising his desire to value people, he shifted to the focus of his management team to the left on the first value by insisting that staff not only value each other, but also that they focus on product quality as a way of valuing customers. He also allowed the team to shift left on the Aptitude scale, shifting slightly away from biasing decisions toward employee's gifts and preferences, toward emphasizing the importance of on-time, on-budget delivery.

The results? While the two managers didn't feel that the rest of the team was leaning far enough to the left, the others felt the pull pretty strongly. The company became more objective in their treatment of people and more willing to insist on production. They went from being marginally profitable to being a very solid performer. Remember that the definition of a healthy company is one that is *both* productive (in this case, that means profitable) *and* where respect, trust, and service flourish.

It's important to note that the culture of the company changed enough through that shift that a group of people felt too uncomfortable about the changes to stay; the company experienced a difficult year for staff turnover. People who were already slightly to the right of the company on those two values, who used to be able to live with the tension, now felt that the gap was becoming too wide for their liking and moved on. Their reason for leaving was not because they couldn't perform well under the new focus on productivity—on the contrary, some of the employees that left were high performers—they left because they didn't feel comfortable with the new culture.

From our experience, we feel that a small gap in values isn't an issue. People who work in an environment that's slightly right or left of their personal values won't experience discomfort. Most people's range of comfortable values on any of the scales is wide enough to accommodate some differences of opinion. As the gap widens, the philosophical differences start to become more obvious. A person who holds values somewhere near the center may not notice that the culture in the company they work for is slightly right of center—there won't be conflict in a small gap. However, move the person into a different company, where the culture is slightly left of center, and the difference will be obvious to them. They won't experience any more conflict in the second environment than they did in the first, but the cultural difference will be tangible.

As the gap widens, philosophical differences become more obvious.

Wider gaps are certain to create discomfort; there's a lot of difference at the heart-level. People on the left of a wider gap are going to feel that the organization isn't as focused on the bottom line as they'd like and is too soft on a lot of issues. People on the right of that gap are going to feel that the organization is too hard-hearted for their liking and will likely feel that a little more focus on the softer side—people's feelings, wants, and preferences—would make things more pleasant. That doesn't mean a wide gap is a bad thing— the execs that the client above added were well to the left of some of the others—but it does mean that the *potential* for conflict runs high. People who are that far apart can work together if they mutually decide that working together is important and necessary for the purpose of achieving a better sense of balance.

There's another dimension along which these value systems flow and that has to do with the fact that we strive for balance in our own lives, whatever that means to each of us. The value systems are arranged in a particular order for a reason, because there are subtle interactions between them that can't be ignored. A person who tends to the right on the Value scale is likely to tend to the right on the scales of Aptitude and Empathy. It's possible that they could orient themselves more toward the center on the remaining two, Learning and Unity, but they're not likely to be strongly to the left. People normally avoid the tension that creates in their own thinking. Whether people live on the left, center, or right, they're likely to live at that point with some consistency.

Value System Interaction

How do the value systems interact? Let's look at them one by one. Keep in mind that a person whose thinking embraces a wide range of a value scale will be much less likely to experience conflict than a person whose thinking preference is focused on a more specific point on the scale. For that reason, we can't say definitely that a gap of a particular "dimension" will absolutely create conflict. Between two people who hold narrow points of view at opposite ends of a value scale, that would undoubtedly be true. Between two people who each embrace a wider, overlapping perspective, there may be no conflict at all.

Value

The wider the gap, the more likely people are to identify differing priorities in terms of taking the needs and feelings of people into account when setting goals and schedules.

Those who lean toward the left—oriented toward tasks and schedules—need to remember that people aren't tools used to get a job done. Failing to value them beyond their ability to produce some sort of deliverable will make them feel used and devalued. Those who lean toward the right—oriented toward people and relationships—need to remember that the whole point of working together is to get a job done. If there isn't some focus on the deliverables, there will be conflict with people who genuinely feel a sense of attachment to meeting the goal and get their sense of fulfillment from completing a job.

To the degree that people lean toward the left on the scale of Value, they are likely to lean toward the left on the Aptitude and Empathy scales. Task-oriented people don't generally have a strong mentoring mindset; they tend to recruit people to their vision more than they try to enable people to discover their own gifts and talents. And, they don't tend toward charity either. Task-oriented people tend to think of the steps that a person needs to take to get out of a difficult situation more than just being there as a support.

The opposite is also true. Those who lean toward the right—toward a people orientation—tend to prefer a position to the right on the Aptitude and Empathy scales as well. People-oriented leaders usually have a sense of how each person in their organization could fit into the various jobs that have to be completed. They're also much more likely to be generous simply because they sense that a person has a need.

When we conduct exit interviews with left-leaning people leaving organizations with right-leaning cultures, they talk negatively about a lack of focus, a lack of commitment to the bottom line, and a lot of wasted money. (Often they add that the wasted money might have otherwise gone to their salaries.) Right-leaning people who leave organizations with left-leaning cultures complain about stress and pressure to perform and about supervisors that didn't care about their ideas and didn't really take any time to get to know them.

Aptitude

The wider the gap, the more likely it is that people will experience conflict over the question of whether or not it's important to take a person's dreams and personal goals into account.

Those who tend to the left in their thinking need to remember that no matter how passionate they feel about their goals, other people are not going to stick with them for long if they don't get personal satisfaction out of working with them. Those who lean left on this scale are likely to have values to the left in the Value and Learning scales too. People who are focused on applying everyone's time toward building a corporate dream also tend to be task-oriented and don't usually have a lot of willingness to invest in what they might see as unrelated training exercises. "We're trying to deliver our product on time and with the necessary quality. What does getting a diploma in history have to do with that?"

Those who lean toward the right need to remember that helping someone find their gifts isn't an overnight exercise, and there might well be valuable life lessons to learn asking them to do things that aren't directly related to what they're particularly "gifted" for. People who have strong coaching mindsets may not see that there is value in learning diligence and perseverance, which are lessons learned by focusing on reaching goals. People who lean far to the right on the Aptitude scale can become manipulative in terms of learning. "I'm your mentor, and I know what's good for you. You just follow the courses and the career path that I've laid out for you, and you'll really be something one day!"

During exit interviews, companies with left-leaning cultures are often accused by right-leaning employees of not caring about their preferences and not being willing to help them find their niche. Employees who lean left, particularly supervisors and managers, who leave right-leaning companies, complain that there's not enough focus on getting the job done and too much pandering to people who are unwilling to shoulder their share of the load. Under the surface, many of them can't really "buy in" to the idea that it is their *responsibility* to figure out how to draw out the gifts in the people they lead.

Learning

A gap here shows up in the expectations around growth and training, particularly in terms of who's responsible to plan, arrange, and pay for it.

The people whose thinking leans toward the left on the Learning scale feel that there's a strong individual component to training—that it's not really their business what other people do to grow and learn, nor is what they are doing themselves anyone else's business. A left-of-center point of view on this scale usually infers that thinking on the scales of Aptitude and Unity will lean left as well. Thinking that how, when, and why people grow is their own business often goes hand-in-hand with very little interest in seeing the potential for growth in someone else's life. For that reason, a person with left-leaning Learning values is more likely to look for ways that others can help them, than in finding ways they can help others. Because they are self-focused in terms of growth, they are more likely to be self-focused in terms of viewing Unity values. To a left-leaning person, fitting with others in a team is not as important as how their present position fits their personal plans and aspirations.

People whose perspective is more to the right tend to feel a sense of responsibility to help others find ways to grow and expect the company they work for to take some interest in what they're doing personally. Leaning to the right on this scale means that thinking on the Aptitude and Unity scales probably lean to the right too. Those who are committed to growth and are willing to help arrange and support growth in others are also much more likely to be looking for opportunities to live out that value in terms of mentoring. When they are focused on facilitating growth in others, people are more likely to value flexibility and try to build synergy in teams.

Left-leaning people leaving organizations with right-leaning cultures talk about patronizing attitudes and a sense that the company crosses boundaries into their private lives. They say things like, "I just work here; you don't *own* me!" or, "You can tell me how to *work*, but you can't tell me how to *live*!" On the other hand, when right-leaning employees leave organizations with left-leaning cultures, they complain about lack of support and opportunity for growth.

Unity

A significant gap in this value system shows up in different ways, depending on whether the person is on the left or right of the gap.

Those on the left of the gap sense conflict about their preference for individual accomplishment. They may feel that the organization wants them to sacrifice their personal goals for the sake of the team—something which they are probably unwilling to do. These people need to remember that what others do often affects what they accomplish themselves, and that others may actually be *depending* on them to make sacrifices once in a while.

We expect that people who lean to the left on this scale will have values for Learning and Empathy that lean left too. When people have strong boundaries in terms of their personal time, they expect others to have strong boundaries too. They aren't likely to violate those boundaries by presuming to tell others what they should be doing with their lives—how and where they should be growing. Their view of empathy is likely to include an expectation that the recipient will take full responsibility for what they've been given and will not resent some sort of accountability for the gift.

Those on the right of the gap will likely sense that there are too many rules and regulations in the organization—rules that they may characterize as "restrictive" and "unnecessary." These people need to remember that policies and structure are an important part of defining expected behavior. On the right side of the Unity scale, people assume that *because they're making sacrifices for the company*, others will too; because they're committed to the company's success, others will be equally committed. In terms of Learning, they're more likely to expect that others will accept input and adjust their plans to fit what's needed by the team and by the organization at large. In terms of Empathy, they recognize that it's important to simply "be there" for others when they have needs.

When employees with right-leaning perceptions leave companies that have a more individual style or culture, they complain that their jobs weren't *fun*. There's no social life within the work environment—the company never facilitates pizza nights or social events. Their spouses never got a chance to meet each other. On the other side of the scale, left-leaning employees leaving companies with more right-leaning cultures complain about how the company consumes too much time building consensus and worrying about what everybody else thinks—not to mention the waste of money on social events that aren't related to work at all!

Empathy

Nowhere are the battles over "right" and "wrong" as fierce as when there's a significant gap between two opinions in this value system. It seems to us that there are many people with strong opinions and personal values here.

We encourage people whose thinking leans toward the left to consider that there are lots of examples where poor planning or bad habits *aren't* the reason for a problem. Life has a way of throwing storms at people, and sometimes it's not possible to be prepared for them or to avoid them. At the same time, we encourage people who lean toward the right to remember that there are times where poor planning or bad habits *are* behind a problem or where a major problem could have been prevented if it was dealt properly when it was smaller.

When we find a person with left-leaning Empathy values, we expect to see a corresponding left-leaning perspective on the Value scale. The belief that good planning will help to manage the "causes and effects" for much of life infers that good planning and scheduling are important in terms of tasks as well. There is also a tendency to lean toward the importance of individual responsibility on the Unity scale.

Right-leaning Empathy values often reveal right values on the Unity and Value scales. Leaning toward charity rather than toward accountability corresponds with valuing flexibility over structure and people over tasks.

It's not hard to guess that when we conduct exit interviews with employees who lean opposite to the culture at the organization they are leaving, we get some pretty intense comments. Left-leaning employees who work for companies with right-leaning cultures "can't believe how much money the company *wastes* on people who are just *welfare cases.*" They can't get over the apparent inequity of the company's willingness to be generous with people who didn't *earn* it, often (in their perception) at the expense of those who did. Right-leaning employees who leave employers with left-leaning cultures "can't believe how *callous* the company is toward people who are having a hard time," and are often visibly angry over the way that the company "let someone down."

Dysfunctional Value System Interaction

People expect that the relationships between the value systems will hold. As we've just described, when people are left-leaning on one value, others expect that they will be left-leaning on most of them. The same is true of a centric or right-leaning perspective. Interruptions of that pattern can often appear dysfunctional. Leaning to the right on four of the values but sharply to the left on the fifth is confusing and counter-intuitive because it's a deviation from the expected norm.

If a company tends to lean to the left—they're relatively productivity-focused and expect people to be fairly independent, then it's expected that that will also have fairly structured top-down decision-making systems, a fairly hands-off policy in terms of career paths and training, a strong set of policies and procedures, and an accountability-based system for employees who encounter trouble in their lives. In other words, no one would be too surprised if the company hands off short-term leave to the insurance company after the obligatory ten sick days and doesn't pay much attention to employees on long-term disability other than to monitor the insurance costs. Someone might be really startled to find out that the company doesn't even have a short-term policy in place, guarantees employees their full salary for the entire term of their disability, and only uses long-term insurance to supplement their costs in carrying the employee's full salary during a lengthy term away from work. It would be unusual and unexpected for them to lean so far to the right on Empathy when they lean left on the other four values.

Here's what happens, and how those counter-intuitive value systems become dysfunctional. Because the company leans left on four of the values, it attracts left-leaning employees. Those left-leaning employees see the company's generosity as being expensive and can't figure out why the company spends money to support people who effectively don't even work there anymore! As a result of the generous Empathy value, employees who would otherwise be happy find that there's resentment building up in their minds, and the health of the workplace starts to degrade. What might have been a healthy organization has suddenly started to develop pain over the inconsistency in the values that they hold to and promote. We've actually heard people say, "The health care policy is unfair—it's biased toward families with lots of kids. You pay $300 per month toward health insurance for a family with five kids, and you pay $150 a month for me, but I'm single. My medical bills aren't anywhere near $1,800 a year, so I must be supplementing the health costs of the bigger family. Can I opt out of the insurance, and you give me the extra $1,800 on my paycheck?"

It's not that the company leans right on the Empathy value system that causes the problem, it's the inconsistency between that value and their left-leaning choice on the others. If the company leaned right on everything, it would attract right-leaning employees who would be thrilled with such a charitable heath insurance system. It's the fact that the choice of value systems is *inconsistent* that causes the problem.

Organizational dysfunction can also be caused by a value system that lives "in the ditch" at an extreme end of the scale. That creates all sorts of problems and becomes unmanageable quickly. If a company is at the left extreme, they may have all the productivity issues solved, and the whole system runs like a well-oiled machine, but the people are being largely ignored. And, because the people are the ones that keep the machine well-oiled, even though it looks like it *should* keep running well, it grinds to a halt when the oil stops flowing. If a company is at the other extreme, they may have the people issues solved, and everybody is happy, but they're not actually *producing* anything! Given that both of those scenarios are more or less self-destructive (they both end in bankruptcy or some other mess most of the time), those aren't the causes of organizational dysfunction that we're most concerned about.

So, organizational dysfunction can come from two sets of inconsistencies:

➤ The horizontal gaps between the values that the organization embraces in its culture and the values that its employees hold to personally.

➤ The vertical inconsistencies where the organization is inconsistent in one value, which makes it stand out from the rest of its culture.

Trade-offs

There's an interesting quirk that we've found as we've analyzed value system alignment. People are willing to make trade-offs. People are willing to artificially live to the left or right of their preferred spot on the value scale, and do it without complaining, *if* they know that the company is making a similar sacrifice that benefits them. An example or two will help.

What about people who do unpleasant or menial jobs? What about the people who pick up neighborhood garbage each week in most of our urban areas? It's hard to imagine that sort of thing being fulfilling and rewarding and yet there are people who do it cheerfully each week. So, what's happening? Most of the workers are willing to trade fulfillment (which is part of Value) for job security (Empathy) and fun (Unity). They have deliberately allowed their employer to push them to the left on the Value scale, in trade for a position which is to the right on the Empathy and Unity scales.

What about people in high-stress jobs? Are they making a trade-off? They're allowing their employer to push them well to the left on the Unity and Value scales in return for a move to the right on Learning and Aptitude. High-pressure jobs tend to have higher rewards in terms of recognition and other perks and often come with a lot of training programs and certifications. People are encouraged to work almost exclusively in their gift areas and delegate almost everything else to administrative staff.

Trade-offs happen by moving a value system *artificially* to the left or right to compensate for an *unavoidable* inconsistency in another value. How those trade-offs work is limited only by the creativity and willingness of the people who have to negotiate them and work with the results. But, trade-offs will only go so far. A wide gap is still going to create significant potential for conflict. Most of us are willing to negotiate for some things, but at some point, our internal value systems can't take the stress of living very far outside of our comfort zone.

The Impact of Leaders' Values on Dysfunction

Twenty years ago, a major oil company with a division of about 8,000 employees had just been through a rather messy acquisition of another company of equal size. At the time, there was a lot of talk about how

139

to integrate the two companies, and a lot of effort was put into trying to find a culture that would work. The president of the division was an older gentleman—gray flannel suit, his thinning hair always neatly cut, stiff black shoes, and a Mercedes to match. Shortly after the integration had settled down into a more or less manageable organization, he retired. His replacement was a much younger man and very different: a brilliant young executive but a bit of a misplaced hippy—Birkenstock sandals, shorts whenever the weather would permit it, medium-length hair, an upscale Volvo, and definitely no neckties! It was amazing to watch the transformation. Within weeks, the *entire division* (including both former cultures, spread through offices in different cities) had begun a massive shift. Things were becoming much more casual. Neckties disappeared; people became much more animated during meetings, and they stopped to talk more in the hallways. What's the point? The personality of the leader has *everything* to do with the personality of the organization, and it doesn't take very long for a new leader to have an impact, *if they are strong enough to influence the culture.*

In small- to medium-sized organizations, the value systems that the leaders believe in and adhere to are usually the value systems that the organization's culture forms around. In larger organizations, "leaders" don't necessarily mean the CEO. Leaders are those who set the culture in their part of the organization. In larger organizations, these could be division leaders, department heads, store managers, or anyone else with enough autonomy to interpret and apply policies and guidelines as they see fit in their part of the organization. A CEO and the executive team may have right-leaning intentions, but if the middle managers who actually implement and enforce policy have left-leaning personal values, it's likely that the message will be moved well to the left before it gets to the rest of the staff.

Some organizational dysfunction starts when leadership changes, and the new leader (or the new influencer) doesn't share the values that the previous leader held. As the culture changes, employees who used to think this was a great place to work start feeling uncomfortable—value systems are shifting, resistance starts to build, and organizational pain starts to occur.

Some organizational dysfunction finds its roots in the fact that leaders have never really thought about being consistent in terms of the value systems that shape the culture and making sure that the culture, and the policies, systems, and processes, are developed around principles that reflect those value systems accurately. As a result, different influencers in the middle levels of the organization are able to put their own values into their own parts of the organization.

Some organizational dysfunction finds its roots in the disagreement between various leaders who don't share common values. If there isn't overlap between their responsibilities, this might not be an issue. But if policies and best practices are written by a left-leaning leader who then attempts to enforce them in a right-leaning leader's department, or vice versa, the results are almost certain to create dysfunction and organizational pain.

Dysfunctional Values among Staff Members

Organizational dysfunction can find its way into the organization when specific individuals don't agree with the company's choice of values even though many of their co-workers do. As people complain and make comments about the company's choice, they start to create mistrust or cynicism. To combat this source of dysfunction, supervisors need to understand that the complaining is not benign and need to start working with the employee to bring about a better understand of the value system or to help the employee transition into a more appropriate position.

Some organizational dysfunction creeps in slowly as new employees are hired. If recruiting procedures don't test for congruence with corporate value systems, employees are hired who simply don't share the values. The assumption is that it doesn't matter; new employees will learn the value system by being exposed to it. Unfortunately, that doesn't appear to be the case. New employees bring their own set of values with them, and if there's a significant gap, the door to organizational dysfunction starts to work its way open. Over time, the views of staff members become fuzzy as different people have significantly different ideas about how things *ought* to be done.

Organizational dysfunction can be stopped if leaders are proactive about sharing the values and promoting the culture they expect. Some employees will adopt the values as their own, others will find that they can adapt, and others will realize that they need to move on—this isn't the right place for them to work.

Dysfunctional Values among Departments

Another area where value system gaps appear is between the value systems and the culture in different departments or divisions. Those differences may or may not create organizational dysfunction. It may be quite acceptable for a research and development division to have a different set of values than the marketing division, for example. Keep in mind though, that employees who make internal moves from one division to the other may sense the change quite distinctly and might struggle to fit in to the new environment.

If two departments need to work fairly closely together, organizational dysfunction is likely to creep in if there's a gap. Unhealthy competition starts to set in, and the departments develop an "us and them" attitude. Issues of *fairness* start to show up. "Why do *they* get that, and *we* don't?" "Why do *we* have to do this, but *they* don't?"

If the organization is small- to medium-sized, we believe that it would be better to have a common, consistent value system and culture that's applied across the whole company.

Summary

It's not possible to keep everyone happy all the time. There will always be people who don't agree with the way that an organization chooses to do things. Just because an organization decides to establish a consistent set of values and works at bringing their policies and culture into line with those choices doesn't mean that everyone will automatically agree with the decision. How does an organization handle the inevitable disagreements? Essentially, they have two choices:

1. Accept the gaps as being an unavoidable necessity, and accept organizational dysfunction as being part of the "cost of doing business."

2. Give people a chance to rethink their own values and decide that they're willing to fit in to the value system and the culture the organization intends to hold to or help them find a new position with a different employer whose values more accurately reflect their own.

The first choice may be acceptable for small gaps, or areas where the disagreements are minor, but it's our opinion that the second option is the wiser choice. How can we know when a gap is significant? We watch for signs of conflict and organizational dysfunction. When organizational pain first starts to appear, the gap is significant enough to warrant management attention.

Organizations shouldn't make the mistake of attempting to modify the value system and the culture if they find a group of people who don't like it. Doing so is to risk becoming disingenuous—untrue to the values that are held—or losing focus. Addressing organizational dysfunction has to be done in keeping with the culture that leaders have designed not the culture that more vocal employees prefer.

In addressing the gaps, beware of what we call Corporate Schizophrenia. That's how we describe situations where companies try hard to embrace different cultures at the same time. It simply doesn't work; it's confusing to employees, supervisors, and the entire management structure. Nobody is quite sure which of the standards applies to any given situation. It is best for companies to be deliberate about choosing a value system, designing a culture, and being consistent in applying them.

Section 3:
Maintaining Organizational Health

If you find some insight in the idea that the five values form the foundation of a healthy organization but don't really have any idea how to implement what you've read, then we haven't lived by the very values that we ourselves espouse. We haven't served you well if we haven't given you something that you can put into practice. In this section, we want to give you a clear and simple plan for putting the value systems into place in your own organization and perhaps even in your own life.

We do need to warn you. though, that these values are not easy to implement. It's almost universally true that if what we *say* does not line up with what we *do*, then we may as well say nothing. Actions always speak louder than words. If we do not have the five value systems functioning at a foundational level in our own lives and our own perceptions and treatment of others, then trying to implement them in our businesses and organizations is pointless at best and hypocritical or disingenuous at worst.

It's taken us months to write this book, and it's taken you days or weeks to read it, but you need to know that building a healthy organization can take years—perhaps ten years if you're trying to turn a dysfunctional organization into a healthy one. This is not the kind of book that you can read, implement, fine tune, and then move on to the next book. This is a book that will radically change the way you live your own life and the way that you live out your values in the organization you lead or work for if you have the courage to implement the value systems personally. But it's also a book that will leave you frustrated if you see its merit and find that you're not able to work through the *personal* change that may be needed before you can genuinely value the people who work with you and for you.

Before you go on to read this last section, you need to ask yourself some questions:

➢ Do you genuinely *value* people? It's relatively easy to value the people who you see eye-to-eye with, but do you *value* the people who tend to disagree with you? The ones who see life differently than you do? Can you value people who you don't naturally like?

➢ Can you embrace the idea that if you will help others find and develop their gifts, and if you'll support them and encourage them, that somehow *your own gifts* will be taken care of? Can you embrace the concept that leadership is about helping others to succeed, not about convincing others to help *you succeed*—that somehow, when they succeed, your success will be found vicariously in theirs?

➢ Do you believe that it's your *responsibility* to facilitate growth in others? Not just an opportunity that you can take once in a while when it jumps in front of you but a *responsibility* that you actually have to put time and effort into. Can you agree that part of your role as a leader is to *actively* find and pursue opportunities to develop others?

➢ Can you see beyond your vision to deliver a product or a service and imagine that you can build a *community*? Can you turn your workplace into a community that people want to belong to? Can you soften rules and expectations and communicate them in a way that tells people you trust them? Can you imagine a day when the people who work with you and for you will say, "Thank God it's Monday!" as they come in the door after a weekend?

➢ Are you able to reach out to a staff member or a co-worker in a time of need and provide gracious and caring support? Can you *give* without strings attached—without expecting repayment

146

or a return on your investment? Can you extend that beyond money or time? Can you extend a gracious *second chance* to a person who's disappointed you or to someone who's made a costly mistake?

Those are tough questions. But they're extremely important questions. The degree to which you're unable to say yes to them is also the degree to which you're going to be frustrated by trying to implement the values we're describing. To change your organization, you may have to change yourself first.

What if you're not the boss in the organization you work for? Can you still use the values to bring health to the part of the organization you work in? We think the answer is a resounding yes! It's been our experience that treating the people around you with respect, trust, and service will encourage them to respond by becoming more open and trusting of you.

Chapter 11: Promoting the Values

By now, we've made it pretty clear that we believe the health of an organization is directly related to how well it finds a place of balance on the value scales. We're convinced by our own experience that profits and productivity are maximized over the long term when organizational health is high.

If an organization is already healthy, and the value systems are consistently entrenched in everything they do, then they just need to keep doing what they're doing! But, because most organizations have some areas of dysfunction, this chapter is going to focus on how to formulate, articulate, and consistently implement the value system.

Be Clear and Consistent

First and foremost, organizations have to be clear and consistent about what they want to do, where they intend to take the culture, and why they believe it's important. They must be absolutely clear in their communication about the importance of having a healthy organization and absolutely consistent about describing what that looks like to them. If it's not clear to the leaders, then it will never be clear to the people they lead or influence. The message has to be internalized—it has to be *real*.

Valuing People is Key

Of the five values, the first is the most important and the foundation for the other four. In communication with everyone, organizations must always be clear that it will value people for more than their ability to produce or perform tasks.

People often find themselves in conversations about others that have a negative context to them; they're disappointed in someone's performance or their contribution, or they're working through a disagreement with someone. When that happens, they need to stop and ask this simple question: "Are we aware of this person's value? Are we keeping the person's value in focus as we have this discussion?"

There are often times when it's necessary to be objective about someone's performance and their failure to meet an expectation. There are also lots of times where it's necessary to discuss someone's character and whether or not they're suitable for a particular role or position. What's *not* necessary (and what must, in fact, be unacceptable) is to *devalue* the person by the way those concerns are discussed.

There's a simple question to ask that keeps the focus on the other person's value: What's the *right thing to do* for *him*? There's something about that question that refocuses the discussion on the individual's value instead of their shortcomings. The questions of the right thing to do for the company or the customer are certainly important and need to be asked, but they shouldn't be asked first.

> *Stop to ask, "What's the right thing to do for him?"*

There clearly needs to be a place for a supervisor to "vent" about a team member who is not pulling their weight or who doesn't seem to fit. It's important, in a healthy organization, that supervisors have a venue for those frustrations and disappointments. But, if discussions with the supervisor end there, he or she leaves with a toxic attitude that spreads the frustration to others. Asking what the right thing is for that team member refocuses the discussion on the intrinsic value of the other individual. The question sends a clear message that the person seen as the source of the frustration or disappointment is still important, despite the frustration, and it's important and necessary to do what's *right* for him.

By the way, what's right for people is not necessarily the same as what's *easiest* for them. It may be that what's right for the other person is to confront them about a poor attitude or some other character flaw that is getting in the way. In some cases, doing what's right for the other person means helping them find a new job! But there's an enormous difference between firing someone to get rid of them when they're annoying and helping someone to find a new job because they're not fitting in and need to find a place where their gifts will be appreciated and where they will have an opportunity to grow.

Part of being clear and consistent means being *authentic* and be *intentional*. Realistically, no one gets it 100 percent right every time. It's likely that everyone finds themselves wishing they'd handled something a little differently. It's in those times that people have an opportunity to acknowledge that they are still working on establishing the values in their own lives and in their own ways of dealing with problems in the workplace. Being authentic means going back and apologizing, and when it's possible, making it right. It means inviting people to point out the inconsistencies between what an organization says and what it does. Being intentional means doing that by design, not by default— planning the culture and not allowing it to form on its own.

Focusing on the values is not trying to change or deny how people *feel* about each other. It is simply a way to remain objective about decisions, basing those decisions on a *choice* to value people rather than on the subjectivity of feelings or emotions.

There's a famous story about President Abraham Lincoln and the man who served with him as Secretary of State, Edwin Stanton, which illustrates the point well:

> On one occasion … Secretary Stanton was particularly angry with one of the generals. He was eloquent about him. "I would like to tell him what I think of him!" he stormed.
> "Why don't you?" Mr. Lincoln agreed. 'Write it all down—do."

Mr. Stanton wrote his letter. When it was finished he took it to the president. The president listened to it all.

"All right. Capital!" he nodded. "And now, Stanton, what are you going to do with it?"

"Do with it? Why, send it, of course!"

"I wouldn't," said the president. "Throw it in the waste-paper basket."

"But it took me two days to write—"

"Yes, yes, and it did you ever so much good. You feel better now. That is all that is necessary. Just throw it in the basket."

After a little more expostulation, into the basket it went.[12]

Lincoln demonstrated that it was possible to value *both* parties; Stanton *and* the general with whom Stanton was upset. By not allowing Stanton to send the letter, Lincoln wouldn't allow him to express his frustration in a way that devalued the other man. At the same time, he expressed value for Stanton's feelings and opinions.

The Other Four Values

Regardless of how difficult it is, keep moving toward the goal. The goal of every business is to maximize profit and productivity—and there's no better way to do it than to adopt a process of continuous improvement toward organizational health. For the most part, "You don't get what you *expect*, you get what you *inspect*." Organizations that want to make progress toward health need to make measuring progress on the value systems a regular part of their management process. Organizations that use a Balanced Scorecard approach toward managing can use the fourth balanced scorecard quadrant, often labeled "People" or "Learning and Growth," to identify those measurements.

Whatever management system is used, the five values are easiest to measure when they are seen with the first value as an overarching principle and the following four values implemented as specific programs or initiatives. Focusing on what's right for the individual with clarity and consistency will increase the visibility of the first value. The management system focuses the organization on the remaining four.

Aptitude

➤ Is there a database that aggregates the gifts and skills for employees? How long is it before a new employee has taken basic tests and can identify their gifts in a common terminology (their Meyers-Briggs MBTI score, DISC communication preference, or WRI bias, for example)?

➤ Is there a correlation between roles and gifts? Can the organization identify the gift and skill mix that is needed for each role?

➤ Are supervisors using that database to determine how they assemble project teams or how they find resources to fill openings? Do human resources staff use the information to screen and select new recruits?

➤ Has character testing become a part of normal selection procedure? Does the organization have a way of testing the character and suitability of potential candidates? Are resume files accessible by the same type of gift and character indicators that are identified for roles?

Learning

➤ Is there a clear system for identifying the employees' growth plans? Does the organization have a way of budgeting training dollars based on their employees' stated training goals, for example?

➤ Is there a system that allows supervisors (who know what an employee's gifts and character qualities are) to recommend that employees take specific courses or training programs to develop character qualities, leadership skills, and communication ability?

> How many employees are actually involved in various training programs? How many are achieving certifications? How many are "dropping out" along the way? Does the organization set a target for the number of employees that are expected to finish a training program and hold supervisors accountable for helping their team members to finish programs or courses so that they can meet those targets?

Unity

> How does the organization measure the level of fun that employees are having at work? While this is certainly abstract, it's not necessarily subjective. For example, is there a budget for social events, and is it being managed responsibly? One of our favorite questions to engage people in discussing this value is, do staff members know what a "win" looks like? Do they know how to celebrate when they achieve one?

> How are new policies created and communicated? Is there are process for ensuring that *all* new policies must be vetted against the vision for the culture before they are implemented? Are at least some of the affected employees involved in helping to write the new policies?

> Does the organization maintain a measurement on an employee's ability to balance their time by watching the average number of hours per week that an employee works? Are supervisors held accountable for keeping that average to a reasonable level?

> Does the organization have a way to quantify inter-departmental cooperation levels? Are supervisors required to share staff members or other resources, for example? How of-

ten does one department genuinely help another department to get a win and then celebrate together when there's a significant success?

➤ How often does the organization help their employees to connect with customers, suppliers, and with each other, in a venue outside of work?

Empathy

➤ Does the organization have a way to detect that there are staff members who have unexpected needs? Are supervisors aware that there is budget available for those situations? Are they commended for using the employee assistance budget when they do so? (We don't recommend penalizing supervisors when the budget doesn't get used—that makes the system focus on the wrong priority. Reducing the need for assistance budgets is fine; refusing to spend them is not.)

➤ Is there a clear process for dealing with mistakes that puts the focus on improving the processes and systems instead of putting blame on a person? Are there forums for open and honest discussion about issues?

➤ Does the organization communicate bad news wisely?

Keep Everyone on the Same Page

Resist the temptation to implement organizational health on a department-by-department basis. What we're talking about here is not a program that the organization is going to implement in an attempt to make the workplace a bit more tolerable. This is effectively a change in the very DNA of the organization itself. The DNA can't be implemented in one department and not another. The best way to implement the "healthy organization DNA" is to do it from the top down.

Beginning with the CEO and the executive team, start the process of asking if you're doing what's right for the person every time a decision needs to be made about discipline or a staffing change. Start measuring the other four values using the regular management reporting process. When leaders begin to hear that employees are raising issues with management about decisions that they see as being contrary to the new culture, there's good progress being made.

One of the first things that need to be done in most organizations is a complete rewrite of the human resources policies, using the value systems as a guideline for knowing how to organize and articulate the policies. Rewrite the policies by focusing on how they support the values instead of how they address potential employee abuses of corporate resources. The next two chapters address that in much more detail.

Practice the Principle of Servant Leadership

We discussed servant leadership briefly in Chapter 3. It's a very workable leadership model that strongly supports the five values and the DNA of a healthy organization. Under a servant leadership model, leaders focus on doing what *only they can do* and leave the rest to the team. While there are things that leaders are *capable* of doing, they choose not to do those things if it's clear that their team can do them as well as they can. They focus on doing only those things that their team cannot do for themselves.

What does that mean in terms of implementing the DNA of a healthy organization? It's our conviction that *anything other* than a servant leadership model has an inherent danger of devaluing people. For example, supervisors who delegate a task but then micromanage are exposing one of several possibilities:

> ➤ They do not trust the person they delegated the task to—there's a fear that the task won't be done well or on time. That

suggests that they haven't taken the time to do proper training or to make sure that their team is properly equipped.

> They fear releasing control of the process. This is especially obvious if the supervisor keeps one critical part of the process under his or her own direct control.

> The fear may be that if the team can do it without them, they have no role left and are afraid their job may be redundant. They don't want their managers to discover that their teams are capable of doing the job without their involvement.

In healthy organizations, the commitment is to *respect, trust,* and *serve* people. If people are not properly trained, and as a result, can't complete a task without a supervisor's assistance, then it becomes the supervisor's primary responsibility to address the training deficit! Without the commitment to training a team to be independently capable of completing their tasks, supervisors can't fully trust team members. If supervisors are concerned with loss of control, they need to change their own paradigm for leadership. A fifty-year-old paradigm for supervisory control of subordinates does not help team members and supervisors to respect each other. If supervisors are concerned that they may be seen as redundant if their team is independently capable, they need to be encouraged to recognize that their skill in bringing a team to capable independence is more valuable to the organization than any contribution they may have made to producing a product or delivering a service.

Serving their team members is the best way supervisors can ensure that their teams serve the customer well. The paradigm that insists team members serve supervisors, policy manuals, and the structure of the organization does nothing to ensure that customers are properly served and cared for!

The most important thing we can say about practicing the principle of servant leadership is that it *must* come from the top and filter its way down the organization. If the leaders at the top of the organization don't serve their executive team, and the executives serve their team of managers, it's unlikely that the model will take root at lower levels of the organization.

Inspect and Correct

To ensure that the process of building a healthy organization takes hold, leaders have to be prepared to make a definite point of focusing on the five values and making sure that they're prioritized in every new policy that's written, and every decision that's made about staff.

Ask the question we posed earlier, "Are we doing what's right for *them*?" much more often than, "Are we doing what's right for *us*?" Insist, for a time, that supervisors or managers vet every decision about recruiting, selection, transfers, discipline, and termination with senior leaders—not so that they can second-guess a supervisor's ability to manage but to ask if we're doing what's right for *them* and ensure that the answer is well thought-out.

For example:

> When hiring, as well as asking, "Are we hiring the right person for the job?" ask, "Are we hiring someone because this is the right job for them?" Has anyone talked to them about why they'd like this job? Have we done our homework—are we going to be getting someone who will enjoy this job? Someone who will have a Thank-God-it's-Monday attitude toward work?

> When the inevitable happens, and someone has to be dismissed, as well as considering the organization's legal protection and other items of due diligence, ask, "Are we doing what's best for them?" Are we, as a company, genuinely serving them by the way that we're letting them go? Are we being generous and gracious? Are we showing that we care about their

family and the impact that this decision is going to have on
them?

➢ As part of regular reviews, hold managers and supervisors accountable for showing value in people. Include metrics on job
satisfaction and create targets for employee survey scores.
Prove to supervisors and managers that the DNA actually matters to senior leaders.

➢ Ask supervisors who recommend a person for a transfer to a
different job or role, "What gifts does this person have, that
make you feel that they'd do well there? What are the gifts and
skills that the new role requires?" Make "gift" a word that everyone recognizes and thinks about.

Create programs and metrics that specifically target each of the
values and implement them as part of the management system. For example, the third value says that everyone wants to learn and grow.
What is the organization doing to encourage people to do that? Are
there specific plans? We'd like to challenge organizations to have every
staff member create a personal growth plan as part of their next performance evaluation. Then, year by year, encourage them to evaluate
and update the plan. Remember that personal growth is not always
going to align with work-related outcomes. There may be a receptionist
who wants to learn mechanics, and a mechanic who wants to take a
course in a foreign language. It doesn't matter—support them and encourage them. When it's appropriate, give them access to education
credits and help to fund their studies. Serve them, and then hold them
loosely accountable for the outcome—use the education credits to
reimburse them for a portion of the tuition, after they complete the
course with at least a 70% average, for example. But don't devalue
them by telling them that their goals aren't relevant. The fact that
people are motivated to learn what interests them helps to keep them
in a frame of mind where they will learn new skills in other environments as well.

To build a healthy organization, focus every activity on building the environment and culture that reflects the chosen value system. Keep everybody on the same page. Be clear and consistent. If you hope that it will happen by default, you will never make progress. Be intentional and focused. Lead by example, and make sure that the example is getting reflected through the entire structure of the organization.

Building a Healthy Culture

In most organizations, culture isn't designed—it's tolerated. While there's often a preferred culture that leadership expects to see on the surface of the organization, there are often pockets of deeply different cultures embedded within the organization itself. In rare cases, the different cultures are the healthy ones—pockets of health in a toxic organizational environment. The more common scenario is that the culture the organization tries to present to the outside world is relatively friendly and stable, but behind the façade there are attitudes and actions that betray a much more hostile culture.

The problem with a toxic culture is similar to the problem the people with character flaws exhibit. It's not possible to hide poor character qualities forever. Eventually, with the right set of stresses or irritants, what's underneath comes through. Toxic management systems can hide behind a cheerful-sounding front counter, but when things get complicated and the customer's expectations don't fit the policy manual very well, the toxicity spills over the counter into the customer's lap.

To establish a culture by *design* rather than by *default*, the organization has to be very deliberate about articulating the characteristics of those interactions and about casting vision for how those environments need to be handled. We believe that cultural errors are much more significant than operational errors. If processes are carefully designed to eliminate the potential for operational error, and there are training programs for many jobs to ensure that operations are conducted safely, efficiently, and profitably, then it seems to us to be equally important that culture be designed and taught with at least the same level of diligence.

The five value systems form the foundation for the culture of the organization, but the culture built on that foundation includes lots of soft qualities that go beyond those values and identify the way that the organization, its employees, customers, suppliers, and community interact. Points to consider are:

> Is the character of the organization politely professional or warm and friendly? How senior leaders deal with managers and supervisors is likely to reflect the way supervisors deal with staff, and consequently, the way that staff deal with customers and suppliers. As long as the choice of character does not conflict with the need to respect people's value, how the organization presents itself is up to senior leaders.

> Internally, how is employee input and involvement recognized? How does the organization express its appreciation? Will employees be singled out for their individual contributions, or will the organization direct its attention toward teams or other groups?

> How available will managers and supervisors be, both to each other and to their teams? Will they communicate primarily in face-to-face conversations, or will they rely on indirect communication, by using e-mail, for example?

We believe that there are many ways for organizations to express their personalities through the culture they create, without compromising the integrity of the five value systems. As long as the foundation remains strong, the expression of individuality is healthy and desirable.

Chapter 12: Building a Road Map

Someone comes home with a new picture they just bought and announces with excitement that they're going to hang it. As soon as they announce their intention, the questions begin: "Which room? I don't think it goes in that room; it's the wrong color. Which wall in that room? What? You have to be kidding! Where on the wall? You can't hang it there; it's the wrong spot!"

Once that debate settles down, the next round begins. "Will you use a picture hanger or a nail? One nail or two?" By the time there are four or five holes in the wall, from moving the nail "up an inch," then "to the left a bit," then "a bit further left," and then "a bit higher," the picture enthusiast isn't excited any more. The enjoyment is gone, lost to the process.

When you first learn about defining a values-driven culture—one that's healthy and is going to create excitement and new life in your organization—courage and new vision often spring up. Like the purchaser of the picture, you return to your organization full of hope that everyone will embrace your new vision. Often, the questions that come from your own team can dismantle the best of intentions in a matter of hours. Momentum is lost, confidence disappears, and your hopes fade.

The process of changing an organization isn't quick or easy. However, it *is* possible. We've watched organizations apply the steps that we're going to give you in this chapter. The organizations that have stuck to the process—followed the road map—have been successful.

For a map to be useful, you need to know two things: where you are now and where you're going next. By this point, we hope that you have a clear picture of where you want to go— the final destination. You want to build a healthy organization. You have a sense of what health means and have started to think about defining the culture you want. You have a clear understanding of the five value systems that define organizational health.

Where Are You Now?

Imagine for a moment the conversations you might have if you walked through your organization and asked people a few open-ended questions about the way that they feel the company treats them. What sort of conversations are you likely to have? How would they respond to the question, "Do you think we have a healthy organization?"

Would the people you ask have a common definition for the term healthy? Would the discussions be positive and energizing or negative and draining? As consultants, we enjoy probing staff members and leaders with good questions and giving people an opportunity to respond in a safe environment. We call it Pulling the Dipstick on an organization. We've found that it's a great way to understand and diagnose what's going on, and it often provides valuable insights for senior leaders who want to know whether things are going as well as they hope or as well as they're being told they are.

Besides interviewing staff, there are three primary tools we use to get a good sense of the organizational health of a new client:

1. A 360° survey of staff members, asking them to provide feedback about supervisors and managers.[13]

2. An interview-based leadership and HR audit, led by a consultant or competent third party. (Doing it yourself is unlikely to been seen as a safe environment and may not get honest answers.)

3. A staff satisfaction survey where respondents remain anonymous.

All three methods are based on the five value systems. Whether we use one, two, or all three methods, we correlate the questions we ask and the feedback we receive to the five values so that we can point directly to the areas where there are issues. By using the five value systems as a framework, we can point to groups of problems that fit into the values and diagnose dysfunction with surprising accuracy.

For each of the five value systems (Value, Aptitude, Learning, Unity, and Empathy), we try to answer the following three questions:

➤ What evidence do we see that tells us this value system is understood and embraced by the organization?

➤ Do we see evidence of principles that tell managers and supervisors how they ought to handle this area?

➤ Are there specific policies and procedures that managers and supervisors follow to implement the principles?

As independent consultants, we've been able to get honest answers in some very toxic cultures and have given our clients helpful feedback and advice that they wouldn't have received if they'd gone out and talked to their staff themselves. (If staff don't trust the boss, they're not about to take a risk by being honest!) To check the organization yourself, you're going to have to find ways of making sure that the people you talk to trust you to be gracious about their input.

Below, we've included a set of typical questions that we use to audit a client's workplace. They're developed by applying the V.A.L.U.E framework to the three questions we ask above. As you go through the questions, think about your own answers: Are you personally engaged in your workplace in a healthy way? Does your workplace offer a healthy culture where you can grow and flourish?

Overview

> ➤ Do you have concerns about the way that the organization treats people?

> ➤ Which policies or people practices are working well? What do you think isn't working well?

> ➤ Over the next year or two, what do you think the organization should be focused on to achieve better organizational health?

Value

> ➤ Does the organization show appreciation for people by listening to their issues, concerns, feedback (positive and negative), and ideas for improvement?

> ➤ Do the people in the organization respect each other? Is there a genuine sense of trust between staff and management and among co-workers?

> ➤ Do you personally feel appreciated by the organization?

Aptitude

> ➤ Does the organization support employees that take personal responsibility for their career development? Can you realistically aim for a position or role and achieve it?

> ➤ Does the organization have a way of matching your gifts to the right area of responsibility?

> ➤ Are you and others held accountable for excellent performance? Is it considered a violation of the culture for a person to do less than their best?

➤ Does the organization invest in young people and help to shape their thinking so that they're prepared to make informed choices about their futures?

➤ Do recruitment and selection processes include an assessment of character and gifts? Do you know how that's done?

➤ Are staff members expected to understand formal character and gift profiles? Is there a standard way of communicating gifts, talents, skills, perspectives, biases, and values?

Learning

➤ Does the organization invest in training? Do investments go beyond skills or job training?

➤ Does the organization communicate openly and honestly, especially with bad or difficult news?

➤ Is there an objective discipline process that gets followed consistently?

➤ Are there policies and plans that look at succession planning and the development of "bench strength"?

➤ How are compensation and bonus programs structured? Do they reward growth or make it risky to try something new?

➤ How quickly do new employees catch the passion for learning and growth?

➤ Does the organization demonstrate by its actions that it supports staff in their desire to grow, succeed, and experience the rewards of growth?

Unity

> ➤ Does the organization have a way of describing its culture? Can it articulate cultural expectations to new employees?

> ➤ Do recruitment and selection processes test for cultural fit? Does the organization have a way of articulating its core values as part of the hiring process?

> ➤ Does the organization invite feedback from staff and create accountability to build a healthy workplace? (By way of an annual staff survey with results published company-wide, for example.)

> ➤ Does the organization maintain time balance guidelines and expect supervisors to administer them?

> ➤ Is there an issues resolution process that allows staff to escalate issues or appeal decisions?

> ➤ Does the organization actively work on building a nurturing, relational, and fun community for people to belong to?

Empathy

> ➤ Does the organization have ways to offer generous and meaningful support for staff members who have personal or family needs?

> ➤ Does the organization have a way to detect that there are needs that warrant their attention?

> ➤ Do staff members have access to professional counselors or support staff?

> ➤ Are the Empathy policies unprejudiced? (Staff who access the programs aren't worried that doing so will cost them a promotion or will limit them in some way, for example.)

When you ask these questions, keep careful track of the answers you receive and watch for patterns of answers from different people that point to consistent problems in a value system. When you find patterns, you'll often be able to address the whole set of problems by looking back at the first section of the book, rethinking your own values as a leader, and then applying a consistent set of principles to the problems you've discovered that are based on the values that you hold personally and the values that you want the organization to reflect.

Planning for the Journey

To begin your journey toward building a healthy organization, you need a clear definition of health for your organization. Our definition, *a healthy organization is a productive organization where respect, trust, and service flourish,* is a good starting point, but you need something that's uniquely your own. If you can't communicate your vision for health in terms that both you and your staff members can understand, then you'll be no closer to a healthy workplace than you are now.

We like to encourage our clients to take what we call the One Month Challenge. Take one month to focus on building a definition for your organization, communicate your vision for health, and start working on building the culture that you want.

Week 1: Build a unique definition of health for your organization

Take a sheet of paper and draw a vertical line down the center of the sheet. Put a heading at the top of each column. On the left, write, "A healthy organization is a productive organization." On the right, write "Where respect, trust, and service flourish."

| A healthy organization is a productive organization | Where respect, trust, and service flourish |

For the next few days, invite several of your staff members, one at a time, to share coffee with you. Let them know that you appreciate them and want their input. Share your desire to have a healthy organization. Explain that you are working on a definition and have a basic outline—a framework definition of health—that you'd like them to contribute specific words and phrases to. The phrases and words they contribute go into one of the two categories. The first category is where you put the words that describe what productive means to the organization. Examples might be: well run, efficient processes, continually improving, etc. The second category is where you put the words that describe what strong, trusting relationships would look like in the organization: friendly, helpful, innovative, etc.

As you add more detail to both columns, work at refining your definition of health until you and the people who have contributed feel that you've come up with a definition that is uniquely your own. By the end of the first week, you've done more that simply create a definition. You've also had a number of conversations that have generated interest, understanding, and a buy-in to the definition.

Week 2: Begin to share the five values with your staff

Host a team meeting, and in your own way, take thirty to forty-five minutes to share the five values with your staff. Use this book as a guideline, follow the V.A.L.U.E. acrostic, and share the message. Let your staff know that each value system plays a key role in driving and developing the relationship and trust side of your definition. Reassure them that business planning, strategy, and execution will continue to drive the productive side of the definition. You might need to encourage some of your staff members to read *Building Healthy Organizations*. The main points for the five values are:

Value: People have inherent value that goes beyond their ability to produce or please.

Aptitude: People's gifts and abilities are an essential part of who they are and what they were destined to do.

Learning: People need to grow if they are to succeed and experience the rewards of that success.

Unity: People need a nurturing, trusting, and fun place to belong to, where they can relate to their peers.

Empathy: People need support to help them get through challenging times.

For the rest of this second week, engage staff members in discussions about the culture of your organization and how the five values help provide a framework for building a strong, healthy organization.

Week 3: Develop a picture of your current culture

Distribute a copy of the questions that we presented on pages 166 to 168. Ask staff members to give you answers to the questions by marking them on a scale from 1 to 5, with 1 meaning they disagree strongly, 5 meaning they agree strongly, and 3 being neutral. (Sometimes a 1 to 10 scale helps people feel that they have more accuracy in giving you an answer—the choice is yours.) It should take each person about thirty minutes to give you their feedback. Have someone on your administrative team compile the results.

When you get the results, spend some time thinking about the areas where the scores weren't as high as you'd like. Which of those areas might you be able to make a significant difference in, with a few strategic changes? By now, you've probably identified a few staff members who have bought-in to the process. Share the results with them and solicit their input.

Week 4: Develop a plan to change one thing for the better

Don't attempt to fix everything all at once. It won't work. If your staff has to absorb a lot of cultural change all at once, the disruption is going to create resistance, productivity will fall, and somebody will pronounce the entire effort "a waste of time." Instead, chose *one thing* that you can put some focus on for the next six months in order to improve your present culture. That's all you need to do to be credible and ensure that your new picture for a healthy organization is put into place with care. More can be done over time, but the first test is always to deliver on the commitment to change *one thing*.

Resist the temptation to pick that one thing on your own and develop your own personal strategy for addressing it! Gather your team around you, present the results to them, share your concerns, and restate your vision for a healthy organization. Then, work toward agreement on which area should be addressed and how.

Taking the First Steps

We often hear from the leaders who attend our courses and seminars that the One Month Challenge seems too simple and too small to make a difference. We agree that it's simple on the surface, but don't underestimate the difficulty of pushing through the changes that you've identified.

The enemy of change

There's a story about Dwight L. Moody, an American clergyman in the early part of the previous century, who was under a lot of pressure from a number of different people. A newspaper reporter, looking for a good story asked him which of those people gave him the most trouble. Moody, without a moment's delay, shot back, "Dwight L. Moody gives me more trouble than any man alive!"

Whether the story is historically accurate or not, the point it makes is clear. We are often our own worst enemy when facing change.

Old habits and natural self-preservation prevent us from changing, despite our best intentions.

To this point, we haven't explicitly stated that below all five values, there's an underlying theme. We've referred to it as balance, perspective, and as reaching widely to embrace other ideas. All of those things are positive ways of presenting a concept that most of us don't initially see as positive at all. In our opinion, it's a principle of life that if you're going to get anywhere, you must be willing to give up something that's important to you before you can expect someone else to give up something that's important to them. The underlying theme is *sacrifice*. When we are willing to sacrifice something that is near and dear to us, others become willing to do the same. That's the fertile soil that trust and respect grow in.

Who is responsible for the present culture in your organization? Whose *personal value system* is reflected in the culture that has formed there? If you are the leader, then whatever toxicity you find in the culture of your organization springs from the values that you personally hold to and exercise, whenever you make decisions or give orders. It may well be true that there are others elsewhere in the organization who have equal or greater responsibility for the organization's culture. However, you can't change anyone else. There's only one person you *can* change, so you have to start there.

Be encouraged. Take the first step. As soon as you start the discussions about the definition of health, you're likely to run into the first opportunity to sacrifice. Can you listen, negotiate, and seek input from your staff members and then give up or sacrifice your own preferences? How do you react when your team wants a different definition than the one you prefer? How do you respond when the first area of poor health you want to tackle isn't even on their radar? Or, when the first area *they* want to tackle is one that points to a potential character weakness in your own life?

We believe everyone is capable but recognize that not all are willing. It takes courage to move forward. Before you feel like the picture purchaser, whose enthusiasm is lost to the process, we have one more tool to offer. Just as there is a methodology to negotiating, there is a methodology to sacrifice. There's no point in sacrificing everything to get nothing. Knowing exactly what to sacrifice and how to do it in a way that gets results isn't a matter of chance. It can be done strategically, deliberately, and with clear focus, and we discuss it in the next chapter.

Chapter 13: Maintaining a Proper Focus

How do you work through the process of change? How do you distill the real issues from the things that aren't important? What's worth keeping, and what needs to be changed? The strategy for making that decision is the same strategy that's behind the way that we've separated a person's preferences from his beliefs and his beliefs from the values that drive his thinking. In the corporate world, it's how we've separated practices from principles and principles from the five values that make up the DNA of a healthy organization. Like most good strategies, it's not complicated. It requires discipline and willingness to make sacrifices, but it's straightforward and easy to teach and apply.

Case Study

One of our clients has a true story that almost everyone can relate to. Rather than just give you the analysis of the technique, we're going to use the story to demonstrate and explain the strategy to you. The names, of course, have been changed—but it doesn't matter, because you can likely put your own names into the story.

Suzanne, a sharp customer service representative has a "chip on her shoulder" over the monthly barbecue. "It's a waste of money!" she says. "People who haven't bought anything here in years show up every month for free food. It costs us hundreds of dollars every month to buy the groceries, and the staff ends up wasting a whole day preparing, serving, and cleaning up afterward. Add it up! It costs us thousands every month!"

Paul, the branch manager, bristles as she dumps her complaints on his desk. He's pretty fond of that barbecue. It's been a fixture in the branch for years, and the whole community knows about it. He knows that some of the people Suzanne says haven't bought anything in years are actually good customers—they don't buy every month, but when they do buy, they buy big-ticket items. Some of them will literally spend a million dollars on a single purchase every few years. That's well worth a few burgers in his mind.

It's a classic conflict that plays out every day in our organizations. If Paul doesn't understand *why* he's hosting the barbecue and can't explain that to Suzanne, he's in an awkward spot. Suzanne has set up the classic win-lose argument. The issue isn't nearly big enough to end up in her dismissal, and she's not going to quit over it either, but it's exactly the sort of thing that contributes to organizational dysfunction. Suzanne finds two or three staff members that agree with her, and for the two or three days around every month's barbeque, they get together and gripe about the waste of money, the waste of time, and how much they dislike having to cook the food and do the cleanup. It won't be long until the people who show up for the event start to pick up the vibes.

To focus Suzanne on why the barbeque is important to him, Paul uses a technique that he learned by focusing on the differences between values, principles, and practices. He understands how to divide the issue into its three parts—practice, principle, and value—and then deals with them as disconnected or uncoupled ideas. This way, he can diffuse the win/lose approach, focus the conversation on the *real issue*, and move forward with Suzanne as a partner instead of an opponent. (We'll say more about how to use this technique below. For now, let's see how it works.)

Paul says, "Suzanne, you know that one of the core values that drives our culture is Unity. We're convinced that it's important for people to belong to a place that's nurturing, trusting, and fun. When we apply that value to our customers and to the community around our branch, we use a principle that says, 'Customers are more than just people who buy stuff. They are an important part of our corporate community, and we want them to feel that they belong here.' Having a barbecue is a practice that we've adopted in order to live out that principle. I can see that you have some really strong feelings about that practice, but I know that you're committed to the principle. If we stop having the barbecue, what practices do you suggest we follow in order to live out the principle of helping our customers feel like they belong here?"

As the leader of the branch—and as the person who is responsible to ensure that there's a healthy culture in his part of the organization—Paul has to make sure that the values are clear and that the principles are respected. He wants to make sure that the Unity value is kept in balance. It's not "all about the customers," and it's not "all about the branch." It's about finding a balance where the customers feel well served, and the staff members feel respected. Customers don't feel like they are smothered by the branch's rules, and staff don't feel like they have to jump to a customer's every whim. Part of the balance is to help customers feel like they're part of the team—they actually *belong* at the branch. Paul's approach, over the years, has been to presume that "getting together" and "sharing food" are the practices that help to ensure that balance.

If Paul is unwilling to make a sacrifice and indicate that he's willing to let "his" barbecue practice go, he comes across as unwilling to consider change. Every leader who hopes to build trust must be willing to sacrifice personal preferences without giving up the principles behind them. Paul shows Suzanne that he is willing to listen to her ideas but that he is not willing to change the underlying principle.

Strategic sacrifices indicate that you are open to change.

Is there a possibility that Suzanne may actually have an idea that works better? Of course there is. It's difficult to defend the notion that that fire and meat are the *only way* to build a community with others! There are probably people in Paul and Suzanne's community that aren't actually interested in a barbecue. Suzanne might come up with an idea that's more inclusive than Paul's!

Imagine for a moment that you are Suzanne's boss. The ball is in your court. What will you do? Do you brush her concerns aside and stick with the old way of doing things? Or will you postpone your comfort, control, and presumptions and allow yourself to weigh and consider her ideas? Now put yourself in Suzanne's shoes. What does it feel like when the boss rejects your idea out of hand, even if you didn't do the best job of selling it?

When we discussed the Value scale in Chapter 2, one of the things that we suggested is that most people don't do what they know is wrong. They do what they *think* is right. Suzanne hasn't unloaded her frustration on Paul's desk because she thinks that her idea is foolish, and she's looking for Paul to confirm her suspicion! She's there because she believes she has a valid concern and wants the branch and staff to do what's right. They may disagree on the specific way to do the right thing, but they actually share a common goal.

It's no wonder that people in organizations everywhere feel the pain of rejection as much as they do. They want to contribute, but the lack of a principle-centered framework makes it impossible for them to do so. Give them a way to contribute—hold your personal preferences and the organization's practices loosely. Be willing to sacrifice preferences and retreat to the principles.

Values, Principles, and Practices

Like Paul, healthy organizations divide issues into their three parts. We actually recommend that they do it graphically. Identify the issue, and then draw three columns underneath it. Label the columns and start the discussion.

Issue: Company Barbecue

Value	Principle	Practice
Unity: We believe that people need a nurturing, trusting, and fun place to belong to, where they can relate to their peers.	Customers are an important part of our business. We want them to feel as though they belong here.	• Monthly barbecue • Clothing with our logo • Customer newsletter • •

Allow people to contribute to the Practice column freely. Whether or not the practice actually changes, the brainstorming process won't hurt and might well generate a good idea or two. Is it safe to let people have input? Everyone will have their own opinion on that question. We think that great ideas flourish in safe environments; they are forged in the crucible of heated discussion and passionate debate!

There will be times when the principles are the source of disagreement. When you sense that a principle is under attack, you need to retreat to the value system and coach staff through the process of either reaffirming the principle or modifying it so that it more correctly reflects the values that are its foundation. The sacrifice here is deeper; it requires that you be vulnerable and willing to put your convictions and beliefs to the test. Allowing someone the freedom to suggest that the principle you hold to is somehow "wrong" or "poorly focused" can be difficult.

There will also be times when your position on a *value* is under pressure. Those are occasions when we encourage you to take time for thought and reflection. Consult with mentors and advisors, decide how deeply entrenched that value is in your thinking, and how deeply you are committed to protecting it. Changing a value system requires the deepest sacrifice of all, and it shouldn't be done lightly. Make it clear that you are being asked to change your character, your thinking, and potentially *who you are*. If the change is necessary, face it with courage. If not, face your opponent with equal courage.

Don't forget that the ones who challenge your practices, principles, and even values are doing so because they believe that they have something to contribute. That doesn't guarantee that what they say is right nor does it obligate you to accept all of their input. It does, however, obligate you to *listen*. Refusing to listen devalues the person who has taken the risk of sharing his or her own thoughts and violates the very values that you hope to promote.

If you think that staff members are suggesting changes purely for "change's sake" remember that the majority of people are highly resistant to change. You can confidently assume that people suggest changes because it's the only way they know to make a difference, leave their mark, or make a contribution. When you realize this, it's easy to see why people take offense or are so easily upset when their suggestions are ignored. As leaders, we are not just neglecting their suggested change, we are taking away their opportunity to make a difference. People who feel they can't make a difference have no real purpose to life—it's no wonder they leave the organization after a while.

Principle-based Policies

How does this apply to the policies in your organization today? In a typical North American business, leaders find themselves pulled back and forth between the needs of the people who work for them, the demands of the marketplace, and often the demands of shareholders. They need to keep costs for recruiting, training, and employee relations to a minimum while delivering increased productivity and enthusiasm.

In that environment, policies cover everything from soup to nuts in an attempt to abide by labor laws and provide a reasonably fair working environment to people who come from a lot of different backgrounds. Most of those policies are written as a result of having to put some sort of rules in place when things were inconsistent, curb perceived abuses, or provide guidance when "common sense" didn't seem to be working.

Think about a typical company travel policy, for example. When an organization is small and everyone does their best to keep costs under control, there isn't much need for a formal policy. When staff members have to travel, they do it as cheaply and efficiently as possible. But, as the company grows and the structure develops, it becomes obvious that there are a few groups of people who think differently about travel. Some staff members travel on Sunday afternoon, have meetings all day Monday, and then fly home that night so that they can be back at the office Tuesday morning. Others think that's unreasonable—they set up their meetings for Tuesday so that they can fly out on Monday (counting that as their day's work), have their meetings on Tuesday, and fly back on Wednesday (again, counting that as a full day's work).

It's not hard to predict how the first group feels about the second. They are probably more than just a bit annoyed that they don't get any recognition for the fact they use their own time to fly and create only half the hotel bills. Why should they make sacrifices when others are *obviously* taking *unfair advantage* of the system?

The two groups aren't arguing about principles. It's not a question of whether there should be travel or not. There is agreement that travel is acceptable and necessary. The arguments are about practices. Eventually, someone writes a policy. People in this job or that job can do this or that. People who report at this level can rent this type of car. The policy starts out fairly straightforward, but things begin to go awry when someone asks, "What if I have to take a client for lunch? I can't do it in *that* car!" So, the exceptions get added. Soon the travel policy is several pages long. The bulk of the document deals with exceptions to the rule and how staff members know if they qualify for an exception. The clerk in the accounting department who has to sort out if somebody qualifies for the expense claim they've submitted needs a law degree to figure it out.

If the people in our example knew how to divide the issue into its three levels, they might have avoided a lot of the fine print in the policy they eventually wrote. For example, what are the values and principles that guide the policy? Using the three-column grid, we can help to guide the thinking. (Feel free to disagree with the suggestions we've made on practices. We fully expect that your own preferences will lead you to different conclusions than our preferences did.)

Issue: Travel Costs and Arrangements

Value	Principle	Practice
Value: People have inherent value beyond what they produce	When you travel, we expect you to minimize expenses and maximize the time you're available for work. We trust our employee's integrity.	• Travel on the cheapest fare you can find. Plan your trips carefully. • Travel that takes less than four hours is not a full day's work. • Check e-mail and phone messages before you leave and when you arrive at your hotel.

Empathy: People need support in difficult times	When you travel, we want you to minimize the total time that you're away from your home.	• Travel outbound in the daytime when you would normally be at work. • Travel home in the evening and take time for your family the next morning.
Unity: People need a nurturing, trusting, and fun place to belong.	You can upgrade your arrangements if it helps you work more effectively.	• Business class tickets for trips of more than five hours flying time, if you do work on the flight. • Upgrade hotel room if you are staying for more than four nights.

From the principles and practices columns, it becomes a fairly straightforward exercise to write the policy. (We've included a sample of the resulting travel policy in Appendix B. It's actually a copy of the travel policy that one of our clients uses, written from the perspective we endorse—based on principles and written from the assumption that people want to do what's right but are just looking for guidelines.)

Mapping policies to principles and values

Each organization will have to develop its own way of describing the values and the principles that the policies are to be based on. What are the principles that need to guide the people in the company? Here's a set that we've distilled from a number of our clients:

Value: People have inherent value that goes beyond their ability to produce or to please.

> ➢ We will be respectful of the people policies give guidance to.

> ➢ Policies will reflect our trust of employee's integrity.

> ➢ Policies will give guidance to decision-makers not eliminate decision making.

> ➢ Policies will be open to feedback (positive or negative) at all times.

Aptitude: People's gifts and abilities are an essential part of who they are and what they were destined to do.

> ➢ We will consistently consider gifts when assigning responsibilities.

> ➢ We will hold staff accountable for excellent performance.

Learning: People need to grow if they are to succeed and to experience the rewards of that success.

> ➢ We will invest proactively in learning and training.

> ➢ We will provide the support and environment for mentoring to occur.

> ➢ We will communicate openly and honestly, especially with bad news.

> ➢ We will treat discipline as an opportunity to correct, not to blame.

> ➢ We will provide regular performance evaluations and feedback.

Unity: People need a nurturing, trusting, and fun place to belong to, where they can relate to their peers.

➢ We will hire based on positive character qualities in addition to skills.

➢ We will keep vision alive and keep staff connected to it.

➢ Where possible, we will involve staff in the decisions that affect them.

➢ We will be reasonable in interpreting written policies.

➢ We will be open to feedback from staff and accountable to build a healthy environment.

➢ Policies will encourage balance in hours worked.

➢ We will maintain a safe and healthy place for staff to spend their time.

Empathy: People need support to help them get through challenging times.

➢ We will provide support for staff in times of personal need or distress.

➢ We will ensure employees have simple and confidential access to support.

➢ We will offer support without waiting for employees to ask.

Feel free to add your own principles to the list. This list just gives you a starting point.

Conclusion

Putting It All Together

It's not magic. Building a healthy organization may not be simple, but it's a practical exercise that every organization can tackle. By understanding that there's a framework of values that provide the foundation for health, every organization can move toward becoming a healthy organization. Trusting, respect-filled workplaces can not only coexist with a healthy bottom line, there's strong evidence to suggest that they can actually *add* to that bottom line.

What Do Healthy Organizations Look Like?

Healthy organizations share a number of common characteristics. They understand that recruiting, selecting, engaging, and retaining the right people requires much more than an attractive salary package. It requires a healthy, trusting, and respect-filled work environment. One of the biggest cost items for an organization is the lack of engagement and loyalty that they find in their staff. Throwing more money at the problem just makes it cost more—a bigger salary and more benefits will never buy loyalty. People want to belong to an organization where they're valued for more than what they can *do*. They want someone to *actually care*—about them and their dreams, challenges, and families.

Healthy organizations are committed to finding a better way to serve staff and customers or clients. For their people practices, they want to move to a values-based approach and away from a rules-based approach. Rules are the antithesis of relationships. Rules are often thought to be objective and fair; relationships are seen as messy. While that may seem true on the surface, the reality is that you can't solve the messy relational challenges by making rules—you actually complicate them when you try. Healthy organizations understand that rules can't come first. Rules too easily become an excuse for neglecting investments in relationships. When you have a rule, you don't have to take the time to understand the situation. But *understanding is what people are searching for.* A values-based approach allows the organization to understand what's really happening and then respond in a way that's appropriate. That's not to suggest that rules are unnecessary or inappropriate. It's just that they shouldn't displace the effort required to understand what's really going on and what's really necessary under the circumstances. The rules have to be guided by the values, not the other way around.

To be healthy, organizations have to understand how to identify their corporate value systems and hire and develop staff whose personal value systems are aligned with the organization's culture. Organizational leaders are well aware of the fact that culture is critical to maintaining a healthy business environment. Yet very few organizations have any idea how to hire based on culture, train people to adopt the culture, and maintain the culture that they want. Healthy organizations know how to do all those things.

Healthy organizations want to help staff move beyond "working for a living" to excited participation in a successful, fulfilling, and rewarding career. Effective engagement is understood to be one of the most important factors in productivity, peaceful employee relationships, and maintaining a stable workforce over the long term. Healthy organizations understand that staff engagement is directly related to health along all five of the value systems. When there's a healthy right-leaning balance on all five of the scales, the staff feels like they're in a place where they *belong* rather than in a place where they're *employed.* People who *belong* don't move on quickly.

Diagnosing Organizational Dysfunction

Organizational dysfunction isn't hard to diagnose. All you need to do is look objectively at the attitudes of the people in an organization to know whether organizational pain is present or not. We're not talking about the one or two people who aren't happy unless they have something to complain about. Usually those are folks whose own value systems aren't healthy, which spills over into their attitudes and perceptions about the workplace. We're talking about the general feeling that you get when you talk to people in the organization. Are they excited and upbeat about their work? Have they bought in to the vision of the organization? Are they fully engaged in what they're doing?

Organizational dysfunction usually shows up first as anger, which then degenerates into apathy—people just stop caring. They feel like the organization doesn't care about them, and so they don't care about the organization either. High turnover rates are another common symptom: people are easily convinced that the grass is greener on the other side of the fence when they feel like their own grass is brown and dry. A third giveaway is high absenteeism rates. When work isn't very engaging, almost any excuse will do to stay away.

Organizations need to look no further than their leaders to discover their values.

Organizations need to look no further than their leaders to know what their value systems are. The decision-makers at the top communicate values "loud and clear" with every decision they make and with every policy they implement. Policies based on values and principles that presume staff are trustworthy, that treat people with respect, that allow supervisors to serve the staff members they oversee, communicate a healthy culture. Rule-based policies often communicate the opposite message.

Healthy organizations work hard at *staying healthy*. Annual trips to the doctor for a physical exam are a good idea for most of us, and they're a good idea for most organizations too. An annual staff survey that asks people to give honest and open feedback without prejudice is the best way we know of to make sure that organizations aren't making presumptions about health that don't reflect reality. Using the staff survey we've provided in Chapter 8 is a great starting point. Set targets for survey results annually and hold managers accountable for their scores. We recommend that our clients set a target of at least 3.75 on the five-point scale. Managers who consistently achieve a 4.00 or better score are doing exemplary work. Those who score less than 3.50 need to take remedial action quickly.

Self-aware managers are key to organizational health. Managers who do the best are the ones who watch their own WRI scores (Chapter 10) and make sure that their own outlook on life stays healthy. When a department scores poorly on the staff survey, we always start with the manager's WRI. Personal value systems are *always* reflected into the culture of the team.

If you find that your own scores are off balance in some way, one of the best strategies that we know of for achieving balance is to find someone that leans the opposite way and forge an alliance with them. Agree to discuss decisions with each other, listening for perspectives and insights. Allow your opposite to pull your scores toward the balance point as you do the same for them.

Developing a Healthy Culture

Never assume that a healthy, respectful culture will develop automatically. If you don't deliberately design and implement culture, you end up with a de facto culture that gets created for you by people who don't necessarily share your values. The culture of an organization either reinforces the values or undermines them.

We recommend that all our clients spend the time and effort to actually write a vision statement for their culture—a set of objectives that they can focus on and measure. Then, treat cultural violations as serious mistakes that are more important than operational errors. Design a culture that reflects the level of respect, trust, and service that you want in your organization, implement it deliberately, and then enforce it firmly. Don't ever assume that customers and clients can't tell within minutes of encountering your staff what your culture is like, because they can and do.

Once the value systems are understood, and leaders are working hard at living out their chosen values, and the culture is taking hold, organizational health isn't far behind.

Servant Leadership

The concept of servant leadership is a fundamentally important one. While there has been lots of talk about servant leadership in the last decade, in most organizations we know, there hasn't been a lot of real change in the way that leaders see their relationship with their staff. For some, servant leadership means "serve until you're in leadership." Once leadership is attained, serving goes out the window. Any leadership model other than servant leadership is incompatible with a healthy perspective on Aptitude and Learning. You can't genuinely be interested in helping others discover their gifts and aptitudes and in encouraging them to grow and develop in those areas if you're not actually prioritizing their needs. That doesn't mean that you have to put their needs first and the needs of the organization second. It means that you have to find a place of balance, where you hold both as important.

A servant leadership culture is critical to a healthy organization. Fifty years ago, people didn't concern themselves with empowerment, self-esteem, and fulfilling work. You were lucky to have a job, and once you had one, society expected you to stay there until you retired. Those aren't cultural norms anymore. The people you hire today *expect* to be treated with respect and dignity. More and more, people are asking, "What's in it for *me*?"

Where Do You Go From Here?

How do you take what you've read and put it into practice in meaningful ways—ways that make a difference for the organizations you are part of today? Begin by making a personal commitment to growth.

Don't resist change—embrace growth as a life-long pursuit. Use your influence as a leader to challenge others to grow too. Ask lots of questions that lead to a place of self-awareness. Becoming aware of imbalance is the first step toward balance.

Remember that balance isn't a matter of picking a specific spot along the value scales and trying to force everyone else to see things in exactly that light. Avoid the "or" and embrace the "and." Reach widely and embrace as wide a point of view as you can, all the while drawing people to a place where they too can see that there's a healthy way to discover balance along the five value systems.

People with a worldview that puts them at the center and makes everyone else serve their needs aren't people we want to be around or form close relationships with. Organizations with the same bias are equally hard to tolerate. We believe that the organizations that are going to lead the charge in this century will be the ones that find a way to balance the needs of shareholders and investors, clients and customers, and their own staff.

Healthy organizations are productive organizations, where respect, trust, and service flourish.

Afterword

Evaluating people's worth based on *who they are* requires that we believe that people have intrinsic value. All people. The ones we like and the ones we don't. The ones that we can relate to and the ones that we can't. The ones who share our ethics, social status, or standard of living and the ones who don't. Our values—our internal guidance systems— have to tell us that people are valuable for much more than *what they can do*. To see that, we have to understand what gives people value in the first place.

We found a story in a magazine about a land reclamation project that illustrates the concept well. This particular property was a ravine that had become an environmental disaster. To start with, someone had bulldozed all the trees, scraped all the dirt out of the way, and turned the site into a poorly designed motocross track. The stream that ran through the ravine had turned everything into a muddy disaster, so the track was of little use. Over time, people had thrown everything imaginable into that ravine—old appliances, tires, boxes of clothing—there was even a broken down moving van full of rotting office furniture! The property was becoming an eyesore.

Eventually, someone came along and saw value in the property that went beyond what was there—they saw the potential. The people who bought the property began by hauling out loads and loads of garbage. Then, they brought in a bulldozer to restore the original contours of the ravine and restore the stream to its original path. They hauled in clay, rock, and sand to restore the creek bed, and replaced tons of soil. Finally, they planted almost 12,000 trees and scattered seed from the native grasses and wildflowers that they collected from neighboring properties. The end result? A beautiful ravine that's likely going to be a favorite spot in time.[14]

Obviously, the renovation added huge value to the property. But, think about that for a minute. What's actually behind the increase in value? Is it the lack of garbage? There are probably plenty of places that don't have garbage in them that aren't as valuable, so that isn't quite it. Is it the trees, grasses, and wildflowers? Again, there are plenty of places that have the same things growing, so that isn't quite it either. The thing that gives the property its biggest increase in value is *that it was made.* Somebody invested enormous effort in the property, and that's what gives it its real value.

If this earth is a giant cosmic fluke, and the emergence of life and the evolution of man is the result of random chance, then *who we are* doesn't matter. Only *what we do* counts—survival of the fittest. But isn't it ironic that nobody wants to be measured that way?

How do we view people's value? Does our assessment go deeper than pure economic or utilitarian measurement? How do we view our own value? Is our self-esteem based on how well we scored in the latest evaluation, or do we recognize that our value lies in far deeper and more abstract qualities?

Those who have bought into a philosophy that equates value with economic or social measures shouldn't underestimate how difficult it will be to change their values in this area! But, failing to change might mean that one day they too become worthless, just more senior citizens putting a drain on the economy fueled by a whole new generation of young, energetic wage earners, who may see themselves as more valuable than those who can no longer contribute.

Endnotes

[1] The Warren Shepell organization makes helpful research available at: *www.shepellfgi.com/EN-US/AboutUs/News/Research Report/index.asp*

[2] NIOSH Publication 99-101

[3] WHO, *Regional Guideline for the Development of Healthy Workplaces*, Regional Office for the Western Pacific, October 1999

[4] For more reading about Servant Leadership, see Robert K. Greenleaf, *The Power of Servant Leadership*, Berrett-Koehler Publishers, 1998; Warren G. Bennis, *On Becoming a Leader*, Perseus Books, 1989; and Ken Blanchard with Phil Hodges, *The Servant Leader*, Thomas Nelson, 2003.

[5] EAP and EFAP programs are systems of short- and long-term disability insurance that help employers to offset the cost of paying salaries to employees who are away from work due to health-related issues, including stress-related absences. EFAP programs often include coverage for employees who are absent as a result of caring for a family member who is experiencing a health-related challenge.

[6] The story has been documented many ways, in many different environments, and is attributed to many different employers, which is why we're simply calling it a corporate myth. If there's a factual event that took place out of which the myth has grown, the leader who made the decision to be gracious about the mistake was clearly someone who had great wisdom and foresight.

[7] Dr. Henry Cloud, *Integrity*, Collins, 2006.

[8] Maxwell, John C. *The 360 degree leader*, Thomas Nelson, 2006

[9] Covey, Steven, *People Centered Leadership*, Simon & Schuster, 1992

[10] Lencioni, Patrick, *Four Obsessions of an Extraordinary Executive*, Jossey-Bass, 2001

[11] The balanced scorecard concept originated in the 1990's as a strategic performance evaluation tool that sought to broaden corporate performance metrics beyond just the financial area. Organizations were encouraged to

measure, in addition to financial outputs, those factors which influenced the financial outputs. For example, process performance, market share, customer service, long term learning and skills development, people practices and so on. The four quadrants of the classic balanced scorecard approach are financial performance, customer satisfaction, internal business processes and learning and growth. Dr. Robert S. Kaplan and David P. Norton's popular book *The Balanced Scorecard* is the classic work on the subject.

[12] Spalding Gerry, Margarita, *Through Five Administrations: Reminiscences of Colonel William H. Crook.*, Harper & Brothers Publishers, New York, 1910

[13] 360° Surveys are feedback and evaluation processes that collect input from a person's superiors, peers, subordinates, and customers. Sometimes, even family members are included.

[14] *Acreage Life*, Western Producer Publications, division of GVIC Communications Inc., June 2005, Volume 1, Issue 2

Appendix A

Confronting with Excellence

Poor Confrontation

Poor leaders use fear as a way of controlling others. They hope their anger will be a deterrent.

Motivation: Anger or disappointment

Poor leaders confront as an emotional response to a mistake or failure. Often, the leaders themselves are embarrassed or upset by the mistake, and confrontation is used as an attempt to restore their control.

Timing: Usually unplanned

Poor leaders confront spontaneously, often as soon as they discover a mistake or failure. They don't take time to consider the situation and understand the context of the mistake.

Focus: On the mistake

Poor leaders focus on the mistake and the results. They presume people were doing what they knew was wrong—either through laziness or noncompliance. They make accusations and dismiss responses.

Purpose: Eliminating mistake

Poor leaders hope that by punishing others for mistakes or failures, the failures will stop. Poor leaders are often personally embarrassed by the mistakes of others—when they confront, they are trying to protect themselves.

Confronting with Excellence

Good leaders create partnerships with others, as a way of inspiring them to grow and improve. Their leadership is based on trust and loyalty.

Motivation: Helping others grow and improve

Good leaders confront as a way of holding others accountable for mistakes or failures, calling them to a higher standard, and helping them reach it.

Timing: Usually planned

Good leaders deal with mistakes in a way that preserves the dignity of others. They try to meet one-on-one and preplan much of what needs to be said, so that even in situations where an immediate response is needed, their words reflect insight and understanding.

Focus: On people

Good leaders focus on the people first and the mistake or failure second. They ask open-ended questions, seeking to understand. They presume that people were trying to do what was right and didn't think before acting.

Purpose: Reiterate vision

Good leaders use confrontation as an opportunity to ensure that others understand their importance. They restate expectations clearly, showing others how their mistakes or failures make it difficult for the team to function well.

Using Discipline

It's impossible to eliminate mistakes. Instead, use mistakes as a leverage point and inspire growth. Repeated mistakes are a bigger problem. Use discipline to eliminate the repetition.

Discipline must be redemptive not punitive. It must be focused on helping others grow, not on punishment. Punishment is a cousin to revenge—it attempts to use fear to control others. Discipline must intentionally be designed to help others grow and improve so that they will be better able to handle a situation in which they've failed previously.

Appendix B

Travel Policy

The company recognizes that travel is a necessary and important part of serving our clients well. Without the right support, travel can be an unnecessarily tough part of a professional's work responsibilities. We're committed to support our staff and enable their success when traveling.

This policy is built on several principles:

➤ Staff will be covered for all out-of-pocket expenses connected with their travel.

➤ HR will keep our practices in line with prevailing legislation and tax laws.

➤ Project managers will be responsible for monitoring and approving travel expenses.

➤ We believe our staff will make every effort to be reasonable and appropriate regarding their travel practices.

Work/Life Balance

Staff and managers need to continually work together to manage and balance time away from home. The number of travel days for our staff will be monitored by HR, and the expectation is that over a one year period an employee will average no more than seven days per month away from home.

Frequent Flyer Support: If an employee has been travelling well beyond the normal expectations during a calendar quarter and is setting out on a trip for more than a week with the trip landing over a weekend, the company will provide the employee with an extra return ticket—either so they can fly home or so that a family member can join them.

Travel Compensation

The company wants to provide staff with the incentive to work extra hours while traveling. In the week of a trip, all hours in excess of forty-five in a week will be paid out at straight time as a travel bonus. A trip does not need to be overnight to have hours from that week qualify for a bonus.

Spending Money for Travel Expenses

If you need a corporate credit card because you travel frequently, your supervisor can request one for you—contact HR for details. Employees who don't have a personal credit card for company travel may find it helpful to obtain a cash advance for the trip. If so, please contact accounting to request the advance.

Booking Your Travel

All travel is to be booked through the company's travel agency. You don't need to involve your supervisor, as he or she will automatically receive a copy of your final itinerary for administrative tracking purposes.

If you need to cancel your trip, please call the travel agency's 1-800 number, which will be printed on your itinerary.

Getting to the Airport

The company will reimburse employees for any expenses related to getting them to and from the airport. Submit mileage claims for your personal vehicle, parking receipts, or cab fare receipts.

Car Rental

Car rentals will be booked with a corporate credit card but will need to be paid for onsite by the employee.

Hotel

An employee on an extended stay may choose to stay in a condo or other accommodation instead of a hotel. That needs to be approved by your supervisor. If you have a hotel preference, let the travel agent know.

Travel Rewards˜

Employees are permitted to keep any noncash benefits received from frequent flyer or other promotional programs. You're more than welcome to use your points to upgrade your travel or accommodation.

If an employee is on a very long flight (five hours or more), and the upgrade cost is reasonable (discuss it with your supervisor), you're welcome to upgrade to business class.

Accommodation with Friends or Relatives

If an employee chooses to stay with friends or relatives at the travel destination and has no hotel expenses, you can double your daily travel allowance.

Daily Travel Allowance

An allowance of $35 per day for each day or part of a day that an employee travels away from their home is automatically added to your expense reimbursement. You don't have to be away from home overnight to claim this.

The intention is to cover the incidental expenses that come up when traveling, such as buying a morning airport coffee, snack foods, a toothbrush, fixing your damaged suitcase, sending your shirts out to the cleaners, or buying new shirts if your luggage gets lost. It also gives you some reimbursement for expenses due to the inconvenience of being away from home, family, and friends.

If you have childcare costs that go over and above the allowance because you're not home, see your supervisor for an override.

Meal Expenses

When you travel, keep receipts for all meals, and put them on your expense account. If you lose a receipt, the company will accept a handwritten receipt for reimbursement purposes.

Appendix C

Mapping Policies to Values

Here is how a healthy organization might choose to relate their people-practices policies to the five values:

Value

➢ Discipline Process
  - o Appeal process
  - o Resignations
  - o Exit interview

➢ Compensation
  - o Pay Scales
  - o Pay days

➢ Bonuses
  - o Certification bonus
  - o Travel hours bonus
  - o Annual average hours bonus
  - o Referral Bonus
  - o Project Profitability Bonus

➢ On-Call Bonus
  - o Policy statement
  - o Formal on-call support
  - o Professional availability expectations
  - o Equipment

Aptitude

➢ Hiring guidelines
➢ Probationary period
➢ Employee classifications
  - o Professional versus administrative

- o Supervisor versus manager
- o Process for determining an employee's classification

➤ Skills Levels
- o Skill level definitions

➤ Career Progression
- o Career progression process

➤ Taking on More Responsibility
- o Moving into supervision
- o Moving into management
- o Role change process

➤ Performance Reviews
- o From the employee's perspective
- o Character
- o Skill

➤ New Employee Training Program

Learning

➤ Training and Development
- o Mentoring
- o Character development
- o Skill development
- o Financial support for training

Unity

➤ Equal employment opportunity
➤ Communication
➤ Issue resolution
➤ Vacation
➤ Statutory holidays
➤ Working from home

- ➤ Expectations of professionals
  - ○ Responsibilities and freedoms of professional staff
  - ○ Flex-time policy

- ➤ Expectations of Administrative Staff
- ➤ Professional Conduct
- ➤ Company Travel
- ➤ Off-site Employees
- ➤ The Workplace
  - ○ Office safety and security
  - ○ Alcohol and drugs
  - ○ Smoking
  - ○ Sexual harassment

- ➤ Expense Reimbursement
- ➤ Retirement Savings Plans

Empathy

- ➤ Benefits
  - ○ Health insurance
  - ○ Healthy living support
  - ○ Employee assistance fund

- ➤ Sick Time Policy
- ➤ Time Off Work
  - ○ Parental leave
  - ○ Grievance leave
  - ○ Other time off with pay
  - ○ Unpaid leave

If you enjoyed this book, you might also be interested in other resources from the BHO Group...

WRI Instrument
The Workplace Relationship Indicator is a values profiling instrument to discover your internal value biases.

Contact us to purchase your copy of the WRI instrument or join us for a half day interactive WRI workshop.

HR Software
We offer web based software to manage recruitment, selection, onboarding and performance reviews. Call or email us for more information.

The BHO Group Contact Information

Edmonton, AB
Suite 200, 10216 – 124 St
Edmonton, AB T5N 4A3
780.454.3700
1.800.359.3758
info@bhogroup.com

Denver, CO
3199 S Wadsworth Blvd Level B
Lakewood, CO 80227-4802
1.866.962.6300
info@bhogroup.com

Visit our website for further information on the BHO Group.
www.bhogroup.com

HR and Leadership Consulting

The BHO Group provides management consulting in leadership and human resources development for business, education, and government. If you have a vision to build a healthy organization or are struggling with staff engagement issues, team conflict or high turnover, give us a call!

Training Workshops

Does your organization have a vision to build a healthy organization but you don't know where to start? We offer customizable education strategies to promote healthy mindsets and behaviors. We also offer the following courses:

- The BHO V.A.L.U.E.s
- Growing Healthy Leaders
- Team Health
- Organizational Health
- Myers Briggs Type Indicator (MBTI)
- Performance Review

- DiSC Conflict and Communication Styles
- Issues Resolution
- Recruitment Training
- Selection Training
- New Employee Engagement

Other good books

There are many other books available in the market today that we recommend on your journey to organizational health.

- The Imperfect Board Member (Brown)
- Leadership and Self Deception (Arbinger)
- Good to Great (Collins)
- Death by Meeting (Lencioni)

- Integrity (Cloud)
- The Four Obsessions of an Extraordinary Executive (Lencioni)
- The Difference Maker (Maxwell)